FROM SOCRATES TO SARTRE,
the Great Mysteries of Life as Explained Through
**Howdy Doody, Marcia Brady, Homer Simpson,
Don Draper, and Other TV Icons**

I Watch, THEREFORE *I Am*

GREGORY BERGMAN

AND PETER ARCHER

Aadamsmedia
Avon, Massachusetts

Published by
Adams Media, a division of F+W Media, Inc.
57 Littlefield Street, Avon, MA 02322. U.S.A.
www.adamsmedia.com

Contains material adapted and abridged from *The Everything® Philosophy Book*, by
James Mannion, copyright © 2002 by F+W Media, Inc., ISBN 10: 1-58062-644-0,
ISBN 13: 978-1-58062-644-6.

ISBN 10: 1-4405-1241-8
ISBN 13: 978-1-4405-1241-4
eISBN 10: 1-4405-2734-2
eISBN 13: 978-1-4405-2734-0

Printed in the United States of America.

10 9 8 7 6 5 4 3 2 1

Library of Congress Cataloging-in-Publication Data
is available from the publisher.

*This book is available at quantity discounts for bulk purchases.
For information, please call 1-800-289-0963.*

Dedication

To the great Steven Ross, a great thinker and an even better friend.

Acknowledgments

Special thanks to Paula Munier, Meredith O'Hayre,
Katie Corcoran Lytle, and Casey Ebert.

Contents

Introduction

"When will I learn? The answers to life's problems aren't at the bottom of a bottle, they're on TV!"
—Homer Simpson

On a cold day in 1884, the patent office in Berlin received an application for a patent from a young man with the endearingly Germanic name of Paul Gottlieb Nipkow. The device Nipkow wanted to patent was called—inventively enough—the Nipkow disk. The disk, combined with other gadgetry, allowed Nipkow to transmit a visual image via telegraph wire, from one place to another.

Sadly, Nipkow's gadget never caught on because no one could see any use for it. Discouraged, Nipkow stopped inventing things and became a railway engineer. But the moment was historic, even if he didn't know it. The Nipkow disk is the earliest version of television. Beginning in the 1920s, other inventors improved the technology involved, and by the 1930s TV saw the advent of broadcast programs. From there, of course, it was a short step to sitcoms, Westerns, dramas, Ronald Reagan, and then a long, dark slide into *American Idol*, endless reruns of *Law & Order*, and *Keeping Up with the Kardashians*.

Right away television raised all sorts of questions:

- Was it a power for Good or Evil?
- Who should control it?
- Could the government use it to control the minds of its citizens?
- How could investors make money off it?

There was a sort of nebulous feeling, especially among the clergy, that television was sinful, distracting parishioners from their more godly pursuits. Others were increasingly intrigued by its ability to shape public opinion. But everyone involved spent a lot of time trying to figure out what this new technology meant. It was rapidly changing the way everyone viewed the world—Vietnam, for example, became history's first televised war. People also started to wonder about how the way we receive information affects the information itself. As Marshall McLuhan said, "The medium *is* the message."

IF ONLY THE GREEKS HAD HAD TELEVISION

It's a curious thing that about 2,300 years earlier, Greeks lounging around on the shores of Asia Minor and the Greek peninsula were asking similar questions. They called their investigations *philosophy*— meaning "the love of wisdom."

The ancient philosophers had relentlessly curious minds. They weren't content to accept things as they were—instead, they believed there was more to the world than met the eye.

For instance, they wanted to know about existence. How do we know things exist? Does something exist just because we think it does? Investigations into this branch of philosophy are called *ontology*. (We promise we aren't going to use a lot of big words like *ontology* in this book. Really.)

They also wanted to understand knowledge—how do we know things? And how do we know we know them? This type of philosophic investigation is called *epistemology*. The word *ontology* comes from the Greek word meaning "that which is," while *epistemology* is from the Greek *episteme*, meaning "knowledge." If someone asks you about that, you can demonstrate how smart you are by spouting out the etymology of these two words.

Finally, they wanted to know how people manage to get along with each other. What convinces us that there are rules we should follow, and what do those rules consist of? They called this inquiry *ethics*.

The ancient Greeks also had a branch of philosophy that today we'd consider to be more the province of science—they wanted to know how the world worked. Was it made of one substance? If so, what was it? What was fire, and where did it come from? What was the cause of clouds? And so on. They called this *physics* or *natural philosophy*.

Some of these questions may strike you as strange or obvious or even silly. But 2,300 years later, we're still asking them. In fact, we've come to realize that the Greeks were really on to something. They may not have had all the answers, but they certainly knew what questions to ask.

This book will tackle some of the most important philosophic questions and schools, using examples from television. Why television? Because today TV is among the biggest sources of information on the planet. More people know who Snooki is than know the name of any great American philosopher. Just consider the following facts:

- There are around one and a half billion television sets in the world.
- The average American watches four hours of television every day.

- In a sixty-five-year life, a normal person will have spent nine years glued to the boob tube.
- The average U.S. household has 2.24 televisions.

Pretty scary, huh?

Television provides a useful reference point too, because it's also concerned with existence, knowledge, and ethics. In some ways, *Jersey Shore* embodies this. If everyone turned off their TV sets, would JWoww, Snooki, and The Situation cease to exist? (God, we hope so!)

Of course, we have to wonder: If TV had been around in ancient Greece, would these guys have invented philosophy? Or would they have spent all their time watching cooking shows about hummus and olives, or game shows like *Athenian Idol*?

Old Herr Nipkow couldn't have known what a can of worms he was opening up with his patent for the Nipkow disk—just as Socrates, Plato, and the rest of the big thinkers in ancient Greece probably didn't realize we'd be discussing these same questions almost two and a half millennia later.

CHAPTER 1

What's the World Made Of? Donuts! And Beer!

Histories of philosophy divide early philosophers into two groups: the pre-Socratics and everybody else. Pre-Socratics are called that because they came before Socrates. (Not too tough, huh? Maybe this philosophy stuff will be easier than you thought.)

The pre-Socratics are also sometimes called the Ionians, because they came from a part of the coastline of what is now Turkey. At the time, this area was called Ionia—so naturally the people from that area were called . . . you guessed it.

See? Philosophy's pretty easy, right? Well, it's a bit more complicated than that.

Some of the Ionian philosophers in particular were important enough that Aristotle (whom we'll talk about later) wrote about some of what they believed. All of them were interested in one of the most important questions of the day: What's everything made of?

Now if Homer Simpson had been around at that point, it's easy to imagine his answer to this problem. Clearly, the most important thing in the world is donuts, washed down by cooling draughts of Duff Beer.

> **"Donuts! Is there *anything* they can't do?"**
> —Homer Simpson

Like Homer, the philosophers of Ionia looked around for the most important thing they could find in their world and then imagined the entire world was made of it.

THALES OF MILETUS

Thales, who lived around the beginning of the sixth century B.C. (the one date that's reliably associated with him is 585 B.C.), figured he had this philosophy stuff down. The world and everything in it, he proclaimed, is made of water. Not only is everything made of it, he said, but it's the original substance that everything else came from in the first place. This isn't completely unreasonable. After all, we need water to live; we're usually not that far away from some body of water (unless you're reading this in the middle of Death Valley or the Sahara Desert).

You can imagine, though, what might have transpired if Thales had ever met Homer—possibly over a drink at Moe's.

Thales: The world is made of water.

Homer: Who's the guy with the funny accent?

Moe: Uh, that'd be Thales. He, uh, he ain't from around here. He's from Greece. He's one of dem philosopher guys.

Homer: Oh, really. Well, let me tell you, Mr. Big Shot Greek Hoity Toity Philosopher Guy that here in Springfield we're patriotic Americans. And we know that everything is made of beer! And donuts!

Thales: [taking a drink of Duff] Beer, you say. Well, perhaps you are right.

Homer: Hey, Moe! We should get Apu in here. This guy kinda talks like him.

Your perception of what the world is made of, in other words, has a great deal to do with what is most important to you. The Ionian Greeks' world was dominated by water—a source of food, drink, transportation, and irrigation. So we can certainly see Thales' point.

THALES WAS A GENIUS!
The human body is composed of somewhere between 55 percent and 78 percent water. Old Thales is sounding smarter and smarter.

Thales' contemporary, Anaximander, disagreed with Thales to the extent that he thought everything comes from some primal substance that's not water. This substance was the basis of the four most important elements: fire, water, earth, and air. Again, this is pretty understandable from our point of view. Thanks to Einstein, we know that matter and energy are different forms of each other—a bit like Anaximander's cosmic "stuff."

Finally, another Ionian, Anaximenes, argued that everything is made of air.

All the Ionian philosophers said, as would many other philosophers, that even though the world *appears* to be made up of many different things, beneath this appearance is a basic unity. This is an important concept in the history of philosophy: What a thing looks like and what it is aren't necessarily the same.

The disparity between form and substance, something that philosophy has spent a lot of time on, is one of the staples of television sitcom jokes. Consider this exchange from the late seventies sitcom *Mork and Mindy* (the show that broke out Robin Williams's career). Mindy, played by Pam Dawber, has been tossed in jail and is talking to her cellmate, Louise Bailey, played by Barbara Billingsley:

Louise Bailey: Funny the way things happen. I'm in here because of a silly old parking meter.

Mindy McConnell: You're kidding!

Louise: No, I went into a hardware store and when I came out, *there* was a policeman writing me a ticket.

Mindy: I don't believe it. They threw you in jail for a parking ticket.

Louise: Well, in a roundabout way. You see when I put the shovel in the trunk, Walter's arm fell out.

Mindy: Who's Walter?

Louise: My husband.

Mindy: What was he doing in the trunk?

Louise: Not much . . . he was dead.

Mindy's made an assumption about reality based on surface appearances. It takes Louise to explain to her the underlying truth of the situation.

Thales, Anaximander, and Anaximenes wanted to go beneath surface appearances and understand the real truth of the world. Once they figured out what everything was made of, they assumed the rest would be easy.

In the same way, Homer tends to assume a simple answer to most of life's problems. This isn't exactly naive—just hopeful.

> **"Here's to alcohol: the source of, and answer to, all of life's problems."**
> —Homer Simpson

This issue of substance versus appearance was taken up in a much more profound way by Plato in his theory of Forms (more about that later).

PYTHAGORAS

Anyone who stayed awake in high school math class probably recognizes the name Pythagoras—wasn't he the guy who made up that theorem? Something about a square on the hypotenuse of a right-angle triangle . . . well, anyway, he had something to do with math, right?

Right. Except that, ironically, he may not have made up the Pythagorean theorem after all. Still, he was the first philosopher to be preoccupied with numbers. He was sort of the sixth-century B.C.'s version of *The Simpsons'* Mathemagician, a party entertainer working with math. Pythagoras must have been a blast at Greek parties.

Pythagoras's basic point is that appearances are deceptive and unreal (remember Thales and company?), and only numbers are real. That's comforting if you're into numbers, but for most of us, not so much.

> **"No! I can't take another minute in the cold unyielding world of numbers!"**
> —Mikey from *Recess*

Actually, a lot of Pythagoras's attitudes about the underlying reality of mathematics played out on the TV show *Numb3rs*. The show's main character, Charlie Eppes, helped his brother Don, who was an FBI agent, solve crimes through applied mathematics.

> **"Some people drink, some gamble. I analyze data."**
> —Charlie Eppes

Charlie, a brilliant mathematician, constantly runs into the problem of the disparity between the elegance of equations and the ugliness of reality. Rather like Pythagoras, he's inclined toward numbers as the true expression of "reality." However, others challenge that rigid viewpoint.

Charlie: Larry, something went wrong, and I don't know what, and now it's like I can't even think.

Dr. Larry Fleinhardt (played by Peter MacNicol): Well, let me guess: You tried to solve a problem involving human behavior, and it blew up in your face.

Charlie: Yeah, pretty much.

Larry: Okay, well, Charles, you are a mathematician, you're always looking for the elegant solution. Human behavior is rarely, if ever, elegant. The universe is full of these odd bumps and twists. You know, perhaps you need to make your equation less elegant, more complicated; less precise, more descriptive. It's not going to be as pretty, but it might work a little bit better. Charlie, when you're working on human problems, there's going to be pain and disappointment. You gotta ask yourself, is it worth it?

Charlie responds by finding ways to adapt his equations to account for human behavior, to try to understand the mathematical realities behind the way things really are. It's a quest of which Pythagoras would be proud.

WHO'S THE REAL MATH WHIZ?
David Krumholtz, who plays Charlie on *Numb3rs*, failed algebra in high school and hated math. Ironically, Dylan Bruno, who plays a math-challenged FBI agent on the show, graduated from MIT with an engineering degree, for which he had to know a ton of math. Just goes to demonstrate the magic of television, doesn't it?

HERACLITUS AND THE RIVER

The pre-Socratics hadn't yet exhausted the topic of what everything was made of. Heraclitus, a contemporary of Pythagoras, thought everything was made of fire. (You can see how the Greeks were working their way through the elements: Thales, water; Anaximenes, air;

Heraclitus, fire. . . .) This led him to an interesting conclusion: Since fire is constantly flickering and changing its shape and color, the only constant is change. Change is the *real* reality, and the stability that we see around us is an illusion. Famously, he said that time was like a great river, and you couldn't step into the same river twice.

Along with this belief, he concluded that the order of things is created by the conflict of opposites with one another, the whole thing controlled by what the Greeks called *logos*, which we roughly translate as "reason."

Let's hark back a moment to *Numb3rs*. The show is really about two brothers, Charlie and Don. Charlie is all mind, the ultimate nerd (although one with a drop-dead gorgeous girlfriend—who's also a numbers nerd; how likely is that?). Don, on the other hand, is the muscle in the family, the rough-and-tough agent who kicks down doors and plunges into crack dens, gun drawn and ready.

And then there's the father, played by Judd Hirsch. He's the voice of reason (logos, if you will), who reconciles the opposites, promotes both their strengths, and makes it possible for them to work together in harmony. That's what Heraclitus was talking about.

You can find this same pattern in other TV sitcoms: the two characters with opposing temperaments, regulated by the calm, wise figure of logos. That was more or less the idea on ensemble shows like *The Partridge Family* (where the logos was played by Shirley Jones) and *Eight Is Enough*, starring Dick Van Patten.

DEMOCRITUS AND THE ATOMISTS

One of the very frustrating things about this early period of Greek philosophy is how much we don't know about it. None of the people we've been talking about left any writings, and we have to guess at their doctrines based on what other people—mainly Aristotle—said about them.

Democritus was probably a very remarkable man, but we don't know when he was born, except that it was sometime around 460 B.C. He traveled a good deal, and this travel enriched his mind. He wrote a book titled *The Little World-System,* which enlarged on the ideas of Leucippus (about whom we know even less than we know about Democritus).

Democritus suggested that everything—both objects we can see and touch and so-called empty space—is in fact made up of tiny bits of matter, so small that they're invisible. Because they're so tiny, they're also compact and thus can't be divided. The Greek word for "indivisible" is *atomos,* so Democritus called his particles *atoms.*

Even though atomic theory was the basis of much of modern physics, Democritus's ideas were far from being in line with today's understanding. We now know, for instance, that atoms can be divided, and that when they are split, there's a release of energy. We know that atoms are made of even smaller particles called neutrons, protons, and electrons and that these, in turn, are made of mysterious things with names like *quark* and *lepton.*

It's interesting that if Democritus and Leucippus hadn't had ideas about indivisible particles 2,500 years ago, we'd never have had TV shows like *Star Trek.* In *Star Trek: The Next Generation,* Lt. Commander Data was always being ordered by Captain Picard to "reconfigure the main phaser array to emit a concentrated stream of chronoton particles." Data would tap a bunch of complicated commands into his control panel, and there'd be an exterior shot of the Starship *Enterprise,* with a weird-looking ray of light shooting out from its saucer section.

Then Data would say something like, "The chronoton ray has been successful, Captain. The asteroid has been destroyed." And everyone'd heave a big sigh of relief and presumably head down to Ten Forward to down a couple of quick shots of Synthehol.

CHAPTER 2
Protagoras, Gorgias, Captain Kirk, and Denny Crane

The pre-Socratics were the warm-up act before Greek philosophy really started rocking the house. The big guns, Socrates, Plato, and Aristotle, were ready to come on stage and do their stuff. But there was one more person of significance before them: Protagoras, leader of the Sophists.

"Man is the measure of all things: of things which are, that they are, and of things which are not, that they are not." This was Protagoras's view, and it would gradually become the basis for most of Western civilization. Judgments, morality, virtues—these are human constructs that originate in the mind. Morality is not based on any objective laws outside of human influence, but is only the product of the human psyche. Morality is man-made.

Today, *sophistry* is a dirty word, at least in philosophical circles. When we accuse someone of sophistry, we mean they're using clever rhetorical tactics to disguise the emptiness of their arguments. (It's a very common insult in courtrooms.)

But among the ancient Greeks of Athens in the fifth century B.C., the Sophists were a respected philosophic school. They were also the first thinkers to charge for their services. Before the Sophists, wise men freely imparted their wisdom, never thinking to ask money for teaching what they knew. The Sophists changed this, and became the first professional wise guys in history, extracting large fees for their services.

The Sophists wandered classical Greece teaching rhetoric, politics, grammar, etymology, history, physics, and mathematics—whatever subject was in demand. They became known as men who could argue any position, however absurd.

Protagoras taught virtue. His somewhat younger contemporary and fellow Sophist Gorgias regarded this as foolish. He didn't believe there was any one thing called "virtue." Instead, he taught what we today would call "situational ethics"—that is, there are many different kinds of virtues, appropriate to different types of situations.

The dangers of this sort of thinking are obvious when we think of the television show *The Practice*, which ran from 1997 to 2004. *The Practice* was about a Boston law firm that specialized in criminal defense cases. Under the leadership of Bobby Donnell, the firm developed two types of defense strategies for difficult cases:

1. **The United States of America defense.** This plays to the patriotism of the jury, emphasizing the constitutional rights of the client and suggesting that they've been violated by the police and the prosecuting attorneys.

2. **Plan B defense.** The defense attorneys push attention away from the possible guilt of their client by suggesting, on very limited or no evidence, that some third person is actually guilty.

The law firm got such a bad reputation for its use of the Plan B defense that it came under increasing attack by hot young idealistic prosecutor Helen Gamble, played by Lara Flynn Boyle. That's the trouble with situational ethics—they can put you in some awkward situations. Gorgias quite possibly found himself in such situations during his teaching. He promised to teach rhetoric, necessary to persuade people, but he never promised what he'd persuade them of.

> "Thus rhetoric, it seems, is a producer of persuasion for belief, not for instruction in the matter of right and wrong. . . . And so the rhetorician's business is not to instruct a law court or a public meeting in matters of right and wrong, but only to make them believe."
>
> —Gorgias

Sounds like today's lawyers.

Gorgias recommended, "In contending with adversaries, destroy their seriousness with laughter." He'd probably agree with the modern legal advice: "If the facts are against you, argue the law. If the law is against you, argue the facts. And if the facts and the law are against you, give the opposing counsel Hell."

Protagoras versus Socrates

We'll talk more about Socrates and Plato in the next chapter, but they come up here because one of the ways we know about Protagoras is from a dialogue that Plato wrote between him and Plato's teacher, Socrates.

In the Platonic dialogue, Plato's Socrates goes toe to toe with Protagoras. This is philosophical debate at its most exciting. The discussion was held at the home of Callias, another Greek guy of importance. A total of twenty-one people are named as present. This was a big deal. Think of it as a WWF title match for smart people.

The main point of contention between Socrates and the Sophist is whether or not virtue is teachable, with Protagoras asserting it is, and Socrates asserting it isn't. From the outset it is clear that their verbal jousting techniques are wildly different. Protagoras, ever the public speaker, drones on and on in what is called "Protagoras's great speech." Socrates complains that Protagoras is long-winded, like a gong that won't stop shaking after it's hit. Socrates prefers short, jablike questions with even shorter answers. The contest ends without a clear resolution, but it gives us a good idea of Plato's view of the two men. He clearly prefers Socrates.

DENNY CRANE—PUPIL OF PROTAGORAS

David Kelley, who created *The Practice*, spun off another show from it called *Boston Legal*, starring James Spader and William Shatner. The latter plays Denny Crane, probably the most arrogant lawyer in all of Boston, if not America. Crane claimed never to have lost a case, with a record of 6,043 to 0.

His self-absorption is basic to his success as a lawyer. To win a case, he's willing to do or say the most outrageous things (like our friend

Gorgias), because winning is everything. "Don't waste your time trying to get into my head," he growls. "There's nothing there." Denny uses his insider connections, particularly with the higher-ups in the Republican party, to call in favors whenever he needs them.

In the courtroom, Crane follows Gorgias's advice about using laughter. Despite—or because of—the onset of Alzheimer's disease, Crane's courtroom antics often carry the day. His outrageousness is matched only by his cynicism.

Compare that with lawyers from television shows in the fifties and sixties: Perry Mason (Raymond Burr) from the show of the same name, Lawrence and Kenneth Preston (E. G. Marshall and Robert Reed) from *The Defenders*, Walter Nichols (Burl Ives) from *The Bold Ones*. These guys stood for something: truth and justice. When Perry Mason defended someone it was because the man or woman was innocent, and we, the audience, could be sure that by the time fifty minutes had ticked by, the truth would be out for everyone to see, Hamilton Burger (William Talman) would see another prosecution case go down the drain (How did that guy keep getting elected district attorney? He *never* got a conviction!), and the real murderer would be shouting from the witness stand, "I did it! And I'm glad! Glad he's dead! Do you hear?"

Gorgias and the Sophists wouldn't have been impressed. In Denny Crane, on the other hand, they'd have found a kindred spirit.

CAPTAIN KIRK AND THE *KOBAYASHI MARU* SCENARIO

Another Protagorean figure whose ethics were virtually always situational was Captain James T. Kirk, commander of the Starship *Enterprise*. Kirk, as he said on more than one occasion, didn't like to lose. The most explicit example of Kirk's obsession with winning occurred in the movie *Star Trek II: The Wrath of Khan*, but it was referred to in several episodes of the various *Star Trek* television series.

In *Star Trek II: The Wrath of Khan*, the occasion for Kirk's win-win focus was the *Kobayashi Maru* scenario, a test designed to reveal young Starfleet cadets' strength of character. In a simulated environment, the cadets must decide whether or not to rescue the crew of the Starship *Kobayashi Maru* stranded in the Neutral Zone between the Federation and the Klingon Empire. Any attempt to enter the zone will precipitate a war between the Federation and the Klingons. The event is set up as a no-win scenario to test how cadets react to losing.

Gorgias in Command of the *Enterprise*

James Kirk was the only cadet in the history of Starfleet Academy to beat the *Kobayashi Maru* scenario. When a young Starfleet cadet, Saavik, asks how he accomplished such a feat, Kirk's answer is straight out of Gorgias's and Denny Crane's playbook:

"I broke into the classroom. Reprogrammed the computers so it was possible to win. Got a commendation for originality."

Saavik: "Then you never faced that situation. Faced death."

Kirk: "I don't believe in the no-win scenario."

DENNY CRANE AND CAPTAIN KIRK: THE SAME PERSON?
A number of novels in the Star Trek series use the *Kobayashi Maru* scenario as a plot point. In the 2009 movie *Star Trek*, directed by J. J. Abrams, Kirk is actually shown using the reprogrammed computers to win the scenario, something that really pisses off Spock, who is an instructor at the academy.

In *Star Trek: The Wrath of Khan*, in which the Vulcan cadet Saavik questions an older Kirk about the incident, Saavik was played by future *Cheers* bartender Kirstie Alley. Kirk, of course, was played by the future Denny Crane, William Shatner.

It seems Shatner has a thing about not wanting to lose.

ZENO'S PARADOXES

It's easy when you think about people like the Sophists to imagine that the early Greek philosophers were just concerned about words. After all, do the kinds of questions that Gorgias and Protagoras were debating thousands of years ago have anything to do with the real world?

As we saw in the case of Denny Crane, they can have quite a lot to do with it. Philosophy has consequences.

However, sometimes you get the impression that the ancient Greeks just enjoyed messing with our minds. Take the case of Zeno of Elea (ca. 490–430 b.c.). Zeno enjoyed paradoxes: statements in which two propositions are each individually true, but they can't be collectively true. If you want to create your own paradox, take a piece of paper and, on one side, write, "The statement on the other side of this paper is true." Turn the paper over and write, "The statement on the other side of this paper is false."

There. You've just created a paradox. If the statement on one side of the paper is true, then the statement on the other side must be false, which means that the statement on the other side of the paper can't be true, but that means that the statement on the other side . . . well, you get the idea.

Zeno's paradoxes were a little bit more sophisticated, and even today, after almost 2,500 years, they can still make your head ache. One of the most famous has to do with distance. You may remember from high school math class that a line has an infinite number of points in it. You can cut the line in half, then cut it in half again, then cut that half in half, and so on. But you can never get to a line segment that you can't bisect.

Got that? Okay, right. Now sit in a chair, facing a door. Get up and walk to the door. If you (or someone else) was able to draw a line between the chair and the door, that line would have an infinite number of points. And how long does an object take to pass through an infinite number of points? That's right: an infinite amount of time.

In other words, you should never be able to get to the door.

> **"That which is in locomotion must arrive at the half-way stage before it arrives at the goal."**
> —Aristotle

Bart versus Ralph

Here's another one of Zeno's paradoxes, this one dealing with motion. Imagine a foot race between Bart Simpson and Ralph Wiggum. Now in the natural course of events, it shouldn't be a contest. Bart's got tons of experience in running: running away from school, running away from his father, running away from work and responsibility. Ralph, on the other hand, is having a good day if he doesn't jam a pencil up his nose. So naturally, we'd expect Bart to win.

Except, according to Zeno, he doesn't. He can't.

The judge for the race (we'll say it's Moe, owner of Moe's Tavern) spots Ralph a five-foot start because of Bart's greater speed. Mo yells, "Go!" and they're off. Ralph takes a stride—more of a wiggle, actually.

Bart, grumpy about having to start behind Ralph, easily catches up to him. But by the time Bart has done that, Ralph's moved ahead another couple of wiggles.

No problem. Bart crosses the distance in the time it takes to yell "Cowabunga!" But by then Ralph has moved ahead one wiggle. Bart catches up, and Ralph's moved ahead by a half wiggle.

And so on. No matter how fast Bart catches up to Ralph, Ralph—pencil jammed firmly in his left nostril—will always be a tiny bit ahead. The amount he's ahead will keep getting smaller and smaller, but it'll never go away, since any distance can be divided into an infinite number of points.

So Bart can never win a race against Ralph Wiggum.

ARISTOTLE AND THE PARADOXES

Aristotle and the great Greek mathematician and mechanical scientist Archimedes both proposed solutions to Zeno's paradoxes, essentially having to do with the distinction between time and space. In more recent times, the paradoxes have occupied a lot of mathematicians, who presumably have nothing better to do than kick around 2,500-year-old problems. Today there's even some debate about whether the paradoxes have been solved, which probably means they haven't.

CHAPTER 3

Socrates:
The Sergeant Schultz
of Ancient Greece

When we start to talk about Socrates, we bump squarely into the problem that although he's one of the most widely known figures in Western philosophy, we don't really know that much about him. He was born in Athens, probably about 470 B.C. He was married, though not particularly happily, and he seems to have preferred to spend time with his male friends. He was reputedly very ugly, although there are no contemporary likenesses of him. He drank only occasionally, but when he did he could consume a huge amount without getting drunk (which made him all the rage at parties).

One of the curious things about Socrates was that whereas philosophers before him had been mainly interested in what the world was made of, Socrates was concerned with human beings. He wanted to know how they thought and how they got on with one another. This laid the basis for the study of what we have come to call *ethics*.

Most of what we *do* know about Socrates comes to us from his pupil, Plato—not exactly an unbiased observer. Plato was very close to Socrates and left us an account of his teacher's death by poison. We also have Plato's dialogue, *The Apology,* which is probably a fairly accurate account of Socrates' speech to the Athenian court that condemned him to death. Apart from that, we have some accounts of Socrates from his pupils. He left no writings, and it's not even clear that he had a systematic philosophy.

So why's he so important?

Because Socrates said that the foundation of his wisdom was that he knew nothing.

"I KNOW NOOOOOOOOTHINK!"

A friend of Socrates once asked the Delphic oracle if anyone was wiser than Socrates. The answer from the oracle was "no." Socrates knew he wasn't wise, so he concluded that his wisdom must stem from the fact that he knew nothing. This was the big revelation in his philosophy: Wisdom is the recognition of one's own ignorance.

Back in the late sixties and early seventies, one of the hottest sitcoms on TV was *Hogan's Heroes,* starring Bob Crane and Werner Klemperer. Crane played Colonel Hogan, an American imprisoned in a German stalag during World War II. Together with a crew of prisoners from other allied countries, he ran a secret operation to aid the Allies and French Resistance fighters right under the nose of the none-too-bright Colonel Klink (Klemperer) and Klink's second-in-command, Sergeant Schultz (John Banner).

The operation worked in part, at least, because Schultz was always determined to ignore the evidence of his own eyes. He would burst into the prisoners' barracks and catch Hogan and his men in the middle of some tremendously complicated maneuver. Schultz would draw up his shoulders, blow on his mustache, roll his eyes to the heavens, and bellow, "I see nothink! Nooooothink!"

Schultz was a sort of primitive Socrates. The latter started from the idea that the basis of wisdom is ignorance. Schultz had the ignorance down; as a result, he tended to see more than Klink, who thought he knew everything going on in the camp.

THE *REAL* COLONEL KLINK
Ironically, Werner Klemperer, who played Colonel Klink, was forced to flee Nazi Germany in 1935. Klemperer only agreed to play the part of a Nazi if the writers would agree to make Klink a bumbling idiot.

Socrates, once he became convinced that the road to wisdom was through recognition of one's own ignorance, decided that the best thing he could do was to explain this to everyone else. In other words, to make other Greeks wise, he had to show them that they, too, were ignorant. Understandably, this didn't make him popular.

CURB YOUR ENTHUSIASM

Socrates' method of investigation of what we don't know has come to be called the Socratic Method. Whereas some philosophers taught by lecturing their students or fellow citizens, Socrates believed that the way to wisdom was through constant questioning. So he proceeded to question everything. No one could make an assertion around Socrates and be safe. He would query the foundations of the statement, the conclusions, and everything in between. He didn't necessarily attempt to construct his own assertions; he just tore down everyone else's. Again, this didn't make him popular.

We can see this method of investigation at work in the television shows *Seinfeld* and *Curb Your Enthusiasm*, both created by and written largely by Larry David.

Let's look for a moment at a typical exchange from *Seinfeld*. George Costanza (Jason Alexander) is defending his lifestyle to Kramer (Michael Richards).

Kramer: You're wasting your life.

George: I am not. What you call wasting, I call living. I'm living my life.

Kramer: Okay, like what? No, tell me. Do you have a job?

George: No.

Kramer: You got money?

George: No.

Kramer: Do you have a woman?

George: No.

Kramer: Do you have any prospects?

George: No.

Kramer: You got anything on the horizon?

George: Uh, no.

Kramer: Do you have any action at all?

George: No.

Kramer: Do you have any conceivable reason for even getting up in the morning?

George: I like to get the *Daily News*.

Rather like George after this bit of dialogue, those interrogated by Socrates felt as if they'd had their worldview invalidated. Nothing they believed in seemed to make sense anymore. And they resented it. They resented having to justify everything they said.

In this sense, Larry David is a distinctly Socratic character. Listen to the following:

Jeff Greene: So, I've given up red meat.

Larry David: Really?

Jeff: Yup, no more red meat for me.

Larry: Good for you. How come you're doing that?

Jeff: No reason.

Larry: What do you mean "no reason"? You gotta have a reason.

Jeff: No, no reason. What do you care?

Larry: Hey, schmuck-face, you can't just say you're giving up red meat, there has to be some motivation behind it.

Jeff doesn't see any good reason why he should explain to Larry his reasons for giving up red meat, but Larry won't let it alone. In the same way, Socrates wouldn't let the assertions of his followers stand until he'd shown them that their thoughts were founded upon shifting sands.

Defining Virtue

For instance, let's look at Socrates' conversation with a young man, Meno. (Plato records this in a dialogue titled, imaginatively, *Meno*.) They start off, reasonably enough, arguing about how *virtue* is acquired. Is it by instruction or practice, or is it something innate in us?

Socrates complains that he doesn't know what virtue means and asks Meno to define it for him. This is the beginning of the end for poor Meno, even though he doesn't know it. He replies that there are many different virtues, appropriate to different ages and circumstances. That's not much help, Socrates replies. If we can't say what all these virtues have in common, how do we know what's a virtue and what isn't?

All right, says Meno. If you want just one definition, virtue is the power to govern human beings.

Not so fast, says Socrates. What about children? They don't have this power. So are children without virtue? And what about tyrants? They exercise that power, but are they virtuous?

Uh, no, responds Meno. How about this: Virtue is the power to do good things and to acquire them. Do you mean, asks Socrates, that there are people who want evil things? Why would they want to do that? If you want something, you want to possess it, and who wants to possess evil?

But what about procuring good things? Meno asks. That's a virtue, right? Sure, replies Socrates, if you think bandits are virtuous. After all, they acquire good things—they just do it at the end of a sword.

The dialogue goes on, but you get the general idea of Socrates' method. And you probably understand how lots of people could and did find it annoying.

THE DEATH OF SOCRATES

During Socrates' lifetime, most of the Greek world was involved in a long, destructive war, the Peloponnesian War (460–404 B.C.), fought between the city-states of Athens and Sparta. As a result of the military turmoil, various political factions sprang up in Athens. One of these, at the end of the war, formed a government known as the "Thirty Tyrants." (Note that in ancient Greece the word *tyrant* didn't have quite the bad connotations it has for us today, but it still wasn't anything to be especially proud of.) After about a year, the tyrants' government lost power, and the people of Athens wanted revenge. One of the leaders of the tyrants had been a pupil of Socrates, and the Athenians turned on Socrates. The leaders of Athens accused him of leading the youth of the city-state astray. He was tried and condemned. He might have lived if he'd apologized, but instead he calmly accepted the death sentence that was handed down. In 399 B.C., at the age of seventy, Socrates was executed by being forced to drink poison.

A DRAUGHT OF HEMLOCK

An episode of *House* features death by hemlock, the poison given to Socrates by his jailers. The victim in the case of *House* made the further mistake of mixing hemlock with steroids. Not a good combination.

If all Socrates did was ask a bunch of questions, piss off a lot of people, drink hemlock, and die, why's he so important?

It's because Socrates shifted the focus of philosophy. The pre-Socratics were interested in whether the world was made of water, air, fire, donuts, or something entirely else. Socrates wasn't, as far as we can tell, interested in these questions. Instead, he wanted to know what made people act the way they did and how they could live together in harmony. These questions were to occupy philosophers for a long time to come.

CHAPTER 4

Plato Is the New American Idol

Good old Plato. He's been called the most important philosopher ever born. The philosopher Alfred North Whitehead said that all philosophy "is a series of footnotes to Plato."

Plato was born into a prominent Athenian political family in 427 B.C. He served in the military during the Peloponnesian War and was briefly involved in some of the political struggles in Athens. As a result, his writings reflect a deeply cynical view of human nature.

He touches on just about every important question in philosophy: ontology, epistemology, ethics, politics, aesthetics . . . the list goes on and on. He began one of the first schools of ancient Greece, the Academy, so called because it met near a grove of trees dedicated to the hero Hecademus. The school became so famous that students from all over the Greek world came to study there.

Plato left a lot for us to use in understanding his philosophy—thirty-six dialogues, which in two fat volumes weigh down any bookshelf. Plato wanted to educate people and believed that ignorance leads to disaster. He was very deeply moved by the death of his teacher Socrates and spent much of his life teaching in an effort to remove the ignorance and suspicion that he believed had led to Socrates' death.

> "Man . . . is a tame or civilized animal; never the less, he requires proper instruction and a fortunate nature, and then of all animals he becomes the most divine and most civilized; but if he be insufficiently or ill-educated he is the most savage of earthly creatures."
>
> —Plato

In the previous chapter, I said that Socrates believed that the beginning of wisdom was the knowledge of one's own ignorance. Plato isn't hampered by any sort of theory like that. He knows a lot and isn't hesitant about communicating it.

THE THEORY OF FORMS

One of Plato's most important contributions to philosophy has to do with how we know things—epistemology. Other Greek philosophers, like Protagoras, argued that knowledge was really a matter of perception and judgment. Essentially, what seems true for you *is* true for you.

Think of *American Idol*. Each one of the hundreds of thousands of contestants is convinced that she or he is *the* American Idol; they tell that to Ryan Seacrest and to the judges. Protagoras, if he were a judge on *American Idol*, would be a little bit like Paula Abdul or Jennifer Lopez—

he'd try to say something good to all the contestants, something to make them feel that what they believe is true: Each one is the American Idol.

Plato, the Simon Cowell of his day, isn't having any of this. He believes that there's a real, objective truth that exists beyond our sense perceptions. This truth is embodied in what are sometimes called "universal notions" like "being," "difference," "good," and so on. These universal notions are also called by Plato "Forms." What we find around us, what we perceive as being, good, et cetera, are only imitations of these universal Forms.

Look at it this way: Ralph, an *American Idol* contestant, appears before the show's panel of judges and announces he's going to sing "Don't Stop Believing" by Journey. He wades through the song, screeches on the high notes, and is stopped after a few moments by Steven Tyler. Randy Jackson tells him he was pitchy, Jennifer and Steven agree, and Ralph stomps through the door and gives the finger to Ryan and the cameraman, who are waiting for him.

A few minutes later, Kelli, another contestant, enters the judging room. "What're you going to sing for us?" Randy asks. "'Don't Stop Believing,' by Journey," Kelli answers.

The three judges roll their eyes at one another. "Go ahead," says Steven.

Kelli launches into the song. Randy stops her. "That was pretty good. I kinda like you." Steven nods. "You definitely got something. I don't know what." A moment later, Kelli comes whooping through the door, yellow ticket clutched in her hand, and hugs her family members.

Both Ralph and Kelli sang the same song. But which one was the real version? We'd probably say, Kelli, since hers sounded better—if by "better," we mean closer to Journey's original version. Protagoras, if he were there, would say both versions are equally real, since both Ralph and Kelli perceived their renditions as good.

Plato would disagree. He'd argue that not even Journey's version of the song was "real." All of these versions are shadows of the universal Form of the song; it alone is "real."

Parable of the Cave

Plato explained this theory in his most famous work, *The Republic*. In this dialogue, he imagines a group of prisoners bound in a cave, facing a blank wall. Behind them is a fire, and between them and the fire passes a procession of people carrying statues of different objects. The fire casts shadows of those objects on the wall in front of the prisoners, so that they think the shadows are the reality. At last, one of the prisoners gets loose and turns around. Now he sees that the shadows were only a reflection of a deeper reality. But he still doesn't quite get it, because he thinks that the statues themselves are the reality.

Slowly he makes his way out of the cave into the outside world. There he sees the objects represented by the statues and realizes that at last he's found reality. (If this sounds at all familiar, it's because it's essentially the plot of the first *Matrix* movie.)

It's easy, as Plato's prisoners did, to confuse appearance with reality. One of the most famous episodes of *M*A*S*H* revolved around this problem. In the episode, Hawkeye (Alan Alda) and Trapper John (Wayne Rogers) invent a fictitious officer, Captain John Tuttle. They use his authorization for anything they want to get away with, as well as assigning him blame for any mishaps.

They're so convincing that before long everyone else in the camp starts believing Tuttle is real.

Henry Blake: I'd sure like to know why it's so sure-fired important for you to see the file on Captain Tuttle.

Frank Burns: Because neither of us has seen him and that strikes us as strange.

Blake: Well, I've seen him. I had breakfast with the man only yesterday. (He pulls out a file.) Here it is. Tuttle. Jonathan, Captain. Serial no: 39729966.

The fake Tuttle becomes so real that he morphs into something of an embarrassment for Hawkeye and Trapper. They kill him off in an appropriately heroic fashion. In the last scene in the episode, Radar O'Reilly (Gary Burghoff) asks Trapper where they got Tuttle's dog tags.

Trapper: Er, that was Major Murdoch.

Radar: Who?

Hawkeye: Who's Major Murdoch?

Trapper: You know Murdoch. Tall, skinny guy. Tuttle's replacement.

Hawkeye: Oh yeah, I had breakfast with him this morning.

Plato aside, sometimes make-believe is a lot more fun than reality.

HAPPINESS IS A WARM PLATO

In *The Republic*, Plato also deals with the ever-vexing problem of human happiness. He says that happiness is a life in which there's a blend of pleasure with wisdom. There are, he further explains, two kinds of pleasure and two kinds of wisdom. Pleasure is divided into:

1. Mixed pleasure, which contrasts pleasurable emotions with unpleasurable ones. For example, when you drink a beer, you're experiencing a pleasurable sensation (the beer coursing its way down your throat) with an unpleasurable one (thirst). Norm from *Cheers* engages in mixed pleasure while at the bar.
2. Unmixed pleasure, which doesn't rely on any contrast. Sam Malone experiences unmixed pleasure whenever a pretty girl walks into Cheers. An unmixed pleasure would be watching a *Cheers* marathon.

Wisdom is divided into:

1. Technical knowledge, which means the ability to make stuff. Woody's ability to make mixed drinks or draw beers is technical knowledge.
2. Cultural knowledge, which means knowing about things like music, art, literature, television, and so on. Diane Chambers has a lot of cultural knowledge, although she lacks technical knowledge, as customers of Cheers soon discover when they order a drink from her.

For the ancient Greeks, the idea of happiness, or *eudaimonia,* is more literally translated as "human flourishing." Greek thinkers like Plato conceived happiness less as an internal state of mind than as an outward kind of excellence, a flourishing if you will. How do you reach this state of flourishing? For Plato, the key word is *harmony.*

All the different elements of pleasure and wisdom should exist in balance. This harks back to Pythagoras and the pre-Socratics, who thought you could find the greatest harmony in numbers. Plato says a life worth living is marked by measure and proportion.

"The man who makes everything that leads to happiness depend upon himself, and not upon other men, has adopted the very best plan for living happily. This is the man of moderation, the man of manly character and of wisdom."

—Plato

TONY SOPRANO MISSES THE PLATONIC IDEAL

The Sopranos started a revolution on television. Loved by critics and audiences alike, this was intelligent, thoughtful writing that kept us on the edge of our seat. The show proved there was an audience for hard-hitting serious television, paving the way for other cable hits like *Dexter, The Wire, Boardwalk Empire*, etc.

Before *The Sopranos*, our image of organized crime was through shows like *The Untouchables*—mobsters wore long overcoats and carried machine guns. Then Francis Ford Coppola, through *The Godfather*, revised that image. Now the mafia was a tortured, dysfunctional family, ripped apart by internal tensions, born of the immigrant experience in America and now sunk in a long, slow decline. *The Sopranos* was a further evolution of Coppola's image.

Tony Soprano heads the Sopranos clan, a modern mafia family. For all their Italian exoticness and deadly criminality, they are just like any ordinary American family. The series starts when Tony, a gangster of the roughest order, reluctantly turns to a psychiatrist because he is having panic attacks.

Tony is a man of many contradictions. He loves his family and wife, but he has an uncontrollable lust for other women. He is a good father who loves his kids, but has not the slightest compunction about murdering a man for business, even if in doing so he leaves a widow and a litter of fatherless kids. He has a hatred of "whiners" who constantly complain about their unhappy lives, yet is equally disdainful of the "happy wanderers" who go through life in carefree, ignorant bliss.

For all his contradictions, he's not exactly confused. Tony knows what he wants and does whatever it takes to get it. If he wants money, he takes it. A girl on the side? He takes it. And if something or someone stands in his way—he deals with them.

Tony is a man in charge. And he knows it. So why does he feel like crap despite his success? As he himself admits, "I got the world by the balls and yet I can't stop feeling that I am a loser."

The Source of True Happiness

By any philosophical definition of happiness, Tony Soprano is unhappy. He says so himself, and rails against the unthinking, blindly smiling masses.

> **"Sometimes, if I see a guy with a clear head, you know the type, always whistling like the Happy Fucking Wanderer. I see this and . . . I wanna walk up to him and rip his fuckin' throat open. For no reason at all. Just go up to him and fucking pummel him."**
> —Tony Soprano

Tony, for all his anti-intellectual bravado, is a thinking man. And the more he thinks, the worse he feels. He shouldn't be unhappy, he reasons, because he has everything that he wants. But therein, according to Plato, lies his problem. Juggling all these disharmonious parts of his life is hard on the soul. It's difficult to reconcile being a family man and cold-blooded killer. Tony just can't do it. He tries and tries but he cannot seem to harmonize the thinking part of his soul, his Reason, with the parts of his soul that are busy eating pasta, screwing chicks, and mustering up the courage for ignoble battle.

This just isn't possible for Plato: "He who commits injustice is ever made more wretched than he who suffers it." In other words, you can't go around being a ruthless criminal and maintain a harmoniously organized soul.

"Excess generally causes reaction, and produces a change in the opposite direction, whether it be in the seasons, or in individuals, or in governments."
—Plato

Tony is stressed because he constantly commits excesses—by killing people, by being unfaithful, by eating too much pasta. And in true Platonic style, those excesses cause a reaction that lands him in the shrink's office. At the very least, Tony's inner struggle creates stress, and stress never contributed to anyone's happiness.

CHAPTER 5

Aristotle Loves Lucy

Among the pupils at Plato's Academy was Aristotle, who was born in 384 B.C. in northeast Greece. After leaving the Academy, he became its most famous graduate, not least because he was tutor to the conqueror of the world, Alexander the Great. He had an extremely orderly mind—in general his thinking seems to be more disciplined than Plato's—and as a result he enjoyed classification. Aristotle knew just about everything that was knowable during his day. Biology, zoology, astronomy, math, logic, physics, poetry, drama—he made major contributions to all of them, and in the case of biology and zoology actually invented them. Like Plato, he founded a school, the Lyceum, which included a library and a natural history museum—the latter of which was started with money supplied by Alexander the Great.

In addition to his attempt to organize knowledge, Aristotle is known for many other contributions to philosophy. Among the most important of these is the field of logic. In fact, we're indebted to Aristotle for many of the rules of what today we call formal or Aristotelian logic.

Formal logic starts with three laws:

• The Law of Identity
• The Law of Difference
• The Law of the Excluded Middle

The Law of Identity is pretty simple. It says that A is equal to A. The Law of Difference simply puts a twist on this and says that A is not the same as not-A. Finally, the Law of the Excluded Middle proclaims that something must be A or not-A—it can't be both. These laws were challenged in the nineteenth century by the German thinker Hegel, but we'll talk about that much later.

I LOVE LOGIC

For right now, let's look at those laws again, this time in the context of everyone's favorite fifties family show, *I Love Lucy*.

In an episode that aired in May 1955, Lucy and Ricky met the great silent comedian Harpo Marx. At the climax of the show, Lucy and Harpo performed Harpo's famous "mirror" routine (originally performed between Harpo and Groucho in the film *Duck Soup*). Each one is dressed alike, and they stare at one another through a large, ornate frame, trying to figure out which is real and which is the reflection.

Now imagine Aristotle, after a hard day of philosophizing, coming home and turning on the television. "Ah ha!" he exclaims to Mrs. Aristotle. "It's *I Love Lucy*, with Harpo Marx! I love this episode."

As Harpo and Lucy stare at one another through the "mirror," Aristotle nods his head. "Of course," he says. "Lucy is Lucy and Harpo is Harpo. Hey, honey! Remember that Law of Identity I was telling you about?"

Harpo and Lucy gesticulate at one another in perfect harmony. The audience can't tell who is following whom—nor, apparently, can Lucy and Harpo. Aristotle chuckles. "It's the Law of Difference!" he says jubilantly. "Lucy isn't Harpo, and Harpo isn't Lucy! Isn't that great, honey?"

Mrs. Aristotle, who has to put up with this sort of thing every night, says nothing, but continues knitting a sweater.

Finally, Harpo and Lucy actually succeed in walking all the way around one another and through the "mirror." They still look exactly alike and move exactly the same. Aristotle gets a slightly worried expression on his face. "No," he murmurs. "No, the Law of the Excluded Middle. They can't be both. Each of them has to be one or the other." He sighs and gets up. "I'll have to work on that some more."

Mrs. Aristotle goes on knitting.

Aristotelian logic is a very powerful instrument, but as we just saw, sometimes its limits are a little, well, limiting. Still, it provided the basis of logical inquiry for philosophers in Classical Rome and throughout the European Middle Ages and into the Renaissance.

SYLLOGISM, SYLLOGISM, WHO'S GOT THE SYLLOGISM?

Aristotle also developed a method of building up a logical construct from interlocking sentences—basic true/false statements. The method is called *syllogism*. Essentially it consists of two parts:

- Premise. There are two of these, and they are simple propositions, stating something about something.
- Conclusion. This follows logically from the premises.

For instance:

Socrates is a man.

All men are mortal.

Therefore Socrates is mortal.

Every day we find syllogisms useful. Consider Stephen Colbert's remark:

"I live by syllogisms: God is love. Love is blind. Stevie Wonder is blind. Therefore, Stevie Wonder is God. I don't know what I'd believe in if it wasn't for that."

FALSE SYLLOGISMS

Syllogisms can be tricky. In the movie *Love and Death*, Woody Allen struggled with this one:

"Socrates is a man.

"All men are mortal.

"Therefore, all men are Socrates."

Well, that can't be right.

THE UNITIES AND *24*

Aristotle's interests also covered drama, which had gotten off to a roaring start among the Greeks with such authors as Euripides (480–406 B.C.), Aeschylus (525–426 B.C.), and Sophocles (496–406 B.C.).

Aristotle dealt with drama in his book *The Poetics*. In it, he developed two rules:

1. **The unity of action:** A play should have one main action that it follows, with no or few subplots. (This does not mean that the plot should be simple and easy to follow. Rather Aristotle writes consistently about the need for the plot to be complex and convoluted.) That said, everything that happens should be intimately linked and interconnected. Subplots just for the hell of it that don't fit into the main action are to be dismissed.

2. **The unity of time:** The action in a play should take place over no more than twenty-four hours.

(A third rule, that the action of the play should occur in one physical space, was added in the sixteenth century by Lodovico Castelvetro, the Italian translator of *The Poetics*, and by the French dramatist Jean de la Taille.) Aristotle should be given creative credit by the producers of *24*.

JACK BAUER: THE ARISTOTELIAN HERO

Ironically, most dramatists don't pay any attention at all to Aristotle's unities—think of Shakespeare, for instance, whose plots wander all over the place. But in the twenty-first century, the makers of the television show *24* decided to rigidly adhere to the rules Aristotle set down nearly two and a half millennia before.

The series starred Kiefer Sutherland as Jack Bauer, a no-nonsense agent for the Los Angeles–based Counter Terrorist Unit (CTU) who took names and kicked ass for eight straight seasons. Aristotle would have loved it.

Each season of the show takes place within a twenty-four-hour time period. The plot of the show is complex, but there is also a cohesive narrative centered around one main action—just the way Aristotle would have wanted it. The show never loses the focus on its primary character and the main action—the most important thing at stake.

Aristotle also stressed that drama should be realistic, drawing from real events or events that could conceivably happen. This means "yes" to terrorism as in *24*, and "no" to vampirism as in *True Blood*. Safe to say that *Honey, I Shrunk the Kids* would not be on Aristotle's top ten list.

Aristotle's Hero

Aristotle was the first to point out that the main character in any story has to be likable—and Jack Bauer is no exception. During its time on the air, *24* and Jack Bauer received criticism for his employment of controversial methods and techniques, including torture, to stop terror threats. Many accused the show of encouraging the controversial foreign policies of President George W. Bush. Despite this, Jack Bauer's willingness to sacrifice himself for the greater good—such as in the episode in which he is willing to give his own life to stop a bomb from killing others—makes him impossible to hate. Even if you violently disagree with this tactics, you know his heart is in the right place.

> **"You can look the other way once, and it's no big deal, except it makes it easier for you to compromise the next time, and pretty soon that's all you're doing; compromising, because that's the way you think things are done. You know those guys I busted? You think they were the bad guys? Because they weren't, they weren't bad guys, they were just like you and me. Except they compromised . . . once."**
>
> —Jack Bauer

Jack Bauer meets the Aristotelian standard for empathetic, likable character—a "good" man. Consistency is also an important element in any good drama for Aristotle. The main character must not confuse the audience through sudden personality shifts. If a character is a tough hero like Jack Bauer, he can't suddenly wimp out in the face of danger. It's all about making sure the story and the character are believable.

Jack Bauer is nothing if not consistent. As viewers, we know he'll do whatever he has to do to get the job done, to fulfill his moral duty. He has an unwavering compulsion to do what he believes is his duty—even if the law interferes with it.

> **"I see fifteen people held hostage on a bus, and everything else goes out the window. I will do whatever it takes to save them, and I mean whatever it takes. . . . Laws were written by much smarter men than me. And in the end, these laws have to be more important than the fifteen people on the bus. I know that's right. In my mind, I know that's right. I just don't think my heart could ever have lived with it."**
> —Jack Bauer

Aristotle, we should note, doesn't have a lot of time for democracy and rule by the many. His ideal government would be an enlightened monarchy, ruled over by—well, maybe by Jack Bauer.

CHAPTER 6
Charlie Harper's Non-Epicurean Lifestyle

By the end of the fourth century B.C., Greek culture had been carried into Asia on the spears of Alexander the Great's army. Alexander died in 323 B.C., but his generals happily split up his empire among themselves and ruled for another couple of hundred years. This period—called the Hellenistic Period—saw the political and cultural center of the West gradually shift to Rome.

ALEXANDER THE GREAT AND HELLENISM

There's no time to go into detail here about Alexander the Great, but suffice to say that he was one of the most important and influential people who ever lived. Ruler of Macedonia by the age of thirty. Conqueror of the known world by age thirty-three. And dead shortly afterward. Now *that's* fast living! After his death, his generals divided up his empire, but they continued to spread Greek culture all over western Asia and as far as the borders of India. This is the cultural movement we call *Hellenism*. (The term comes from the Greek *Hellen*, the word the Greeks used to describe themselves.)

The Romans were a lot more practical than the Greeks. Whereas the Greeks sat around debating annoyingly abstract issues like "virtue" and "being," the Romans were more concerned with running not only their state but, in a few hundred years, the biggest empire in the world. Still, they were very interested in philosophy and looked to the Greeks for ideas.

Two schools of Greek philosophy, which grew up during the Hellenistic period, developed extensive followings in Rome: the Epicureans and the Stoics.

WHO'S THE EPICUREAN?

Think about Charlie Harper from *Two and a Half Men*. He drinks, smokes cigars, eats pizza, and sleeps with every beautiful woman he lays eyes—and anything else he can manage—on. He's got a job writing jingles (later this morphs into writing kids' songs) that provides him with all the money he needs. He spends his nights carousing with gorgeous women who have self-esteem issues and his days sleeping off hangovers.

In contrast, his brother Alan is a struggling chiropractor paying alimony to a shrewish ex-wife and trying to cope with his none-too-bright kid on the weekends. Alan's so tightly wound that his stomach is perpetually wrapped around his backbone. Unlike Charlie, he almost never has any fun and rarely gets lucky. Alan's idea of a fun evening is to sit at home with a good book or watch the Nature channel on television. Not that he'll be able to do that without some harassment from his brother.

Charlie: Hey. After the kid goes back to his mother's, do you wanna go out and grab some dinner?

Alan: I can't go out to dinner, Charlie.

Charlie: Why not? You got a date—he said, knowing the answer, but asked him anyway just to be polite.

Alan: No, I don't have a date—he replied, all the while thinking: "Bite me, you booze-addled buffoon."

Most people would probably say that the Epicureans would have approved of Charlie. Their founder, Epicurus, was born around 341 B.C. on the island of Samos. Supposedly he wrote more than 300 books, but we only have fragments of them today. As is the case with most Greek philosophers, what we know about Epicurus comes to us from other people. He wrote about physics (that is, the natural world) and philosophic method, but it's his writing about ethics that interests us here.

Epicurus starts out from the idea that pleasure is good.

"For we recognize pleasure as the first good in us, and from pleasure we begin every act of choice and avoidance, and to pleasure we return again, using the feeling as the standard by which we judge every good."
—Epicurus

Active and Static Pleasures

But, Epicurus says, there are different kinds of pleasure. He distinguishes between "active" pleasure, which we indulge in to gratify a need or desire, and "static" pleasure, which is independent of desire. From his point of view, "active" pleasure is limited by the extent of the need that produces it.

For instance: Charlie Harper is thirsty. He knows what'll cure this: beer. He goes to the kitchen, exchanges some backchat with Berta the housekeeper, and gets a beer out of the fridge. He settles down on the couch to drink it and is joined first by Jake ("What's on, Uncle Charlie?" "Whaddya want to watch?" "Depends what's on?" "Depends on what you wanna watch." "Well, I don't know what I wanna watch until I know what's on.") and then Alan ("Ooo! Look! PBS is showing a documentary about the life of snails!").

Charlie finishes his beer. He isn't thirsty anymore. He has taken pleasure from removing that need for beer. But here's the problem, according to Epicurus: Having taken away the desire, Charlie can't continue to enjoy the pleasure. After all, he can't be less thirsty than not thirsty. So his pleasure is at an end—the more so since Jake and Alan are now sprawled out across the sofa, fighting over the TV remote.

Alan, in contrast, takes pleasure from improving his mind by watching a documentary about snails. (Jake, when it becomes clear that this is going to be the program they're going to watch, goes off to his room for some privacy—and in the context of a teenage boy, we all know what that means.) Alan doesn't have a need to learn about snails; he simply enjoys improving his mind. Epicurus would argue that there's no limitation on this, and Alan's pleasure can go on forever. Thus Alan's pleasure is superior to Charlie's, and Alan is the true Epicurean.

EPICUREAN MISUNDERSTANDINGS

Down through the ages, Epicurus's philosophy has been misinterpreted to mean that he encouraged any and all kinds of pleasure, especially ones that involved eating, drinking, and having lots of sex. One result is our word *epicurean*, which means someone who has luxurious tastes, especially in regard to eating and drinking. Epicurus would have been horrified by this misunderstanding.

THE STOIC MR. SPOCK

Zeno of Citium, who was born about 336 B.C. on Cyprus, was the originator of Stoicism. He used to give lectures to students while standing on the colonnade or porch of a temple; the word in Greek for "porch" is *stoa*, hence Stoicism.

Zeno and the Stoics believed the goal of philosophy—and of life—was to attain a serenity and peacefulness of mind, a feat acquired by living a life of virtue.

This life, they said, should be lived in accord with divine law, which in turn was in accord with Nature. This idea is expressed by the Greek word *logos*, which is the root of our word "logic." But whereas by logic we mean a clear habit of thought, the Greeks gave it a broader meaning. The Stoics made logos into a lifestyle.

If this is starting to sound familiar to you, it's because viewers of American television in the 1960s (and later in the movies) met someone who ordered his life by logic: *Star Trek*'s Mr. Spock.

Spock was played in the series by Leonard Nimoy. Considering the revolutionary nature of the show it's something of a miracle that it got made at all, let alone that it grew in popularity until it was a genuine cultural phenomenon. After viewing early episodes, one unnamed NBC executive advised creator Gene Roddenberry to "get rid of the pointy-eared guy." Fortunately, Roddenberry ignored the suggestion.

> **"I realize this is a hard choice, Captain, but the needs of the many must outweigh the needs of the few."**
> —Mr. Spock

If the Stoic ideal is the ability to make rational decisions independent from your emotions, then Mr. Spock of Starfleet is your man . . . well, half man and half Vulcan anyway.

Spock is all brain. Flaunting his superhuman intelligence, he can assess a situation with a level of accuracy and specificity that would have made Zeno swoon. His unemotional logic is constantly contrasted by the show's writers with Dr. Leonard McCoy, who invariably gets angry at Spock's bloodless approach to any problem.

Spock's human side comes from his mother, who, in one of the first interspecies marriages in *Star Trek*, was wed to the Vulcan leader Sarek.

Spock: Emotional, isn't she?

Sarek: She has always been so.

Spock: Why did you marry her?

Sarek: It seemed the logical thing to do at the time.

Keep in mind that this is Spock's own *mother* he's talking about. He's just as capable of calmly, logically evaluating emotional relationships as he would be about calculating a planet's orbit.

But—and here's why Spock is a great example of a Stoic personality—Vulcans aren't naturally unemotional and logical. In fact, they have very strong emotions, which they consciously keep in check. Spock, in other words, has much more in common with McCoy than he might care to admit.

The Vulcans became convinced, early in their history, that emotions were highly destructive, particularly if unchecked. As a result, they practice complex techniques to keep their own emotional impulses in check. They strive for a state of pure logic, through which they find tranquility. The most advanced form of this is the ritual *Kolinahr* through which Vulcans attain an emotion-free state (Spock, by the way, never gets to this point, although he has a shot at it in the beginning of *Star Trek: The Motion Picture*).

The Greeks called this tranquility *apathia* (from which we get the word *apathy*). It means the eradication of illogical emotions and passions. Spock would have been quite at home at Zeno's house on a Saturday evening.

> **"Do not spoil what you have by desiring what you have not; remember that what you now have was once among the things you only hoped for."**
> —Epicurus

Epicurus believed that to achieve true happiness, one should try to live a peaceful, obscure life. (Alan Harper in *Two and a Half Men* is certainly doing this, albeit not voluntarily.) Zeno, on the other hand, thought that living in accord with logos related humans to one another; consequently we should live for one another. Spock expresses this notion perfectly when he says, "The needs of the many outweigh the needs of the few." You can understand why, with this outlook, Stoicism became the favorite philosophy of the Roman Empire.

One of the most important virtues to the Stoics is independence. Diogenes and his fellow Cynics—from whom the Stoics derived the basis of many of their ideas—preached an independence from material things, favoring simple living over luxury. Diogenes practiced what he preached, and is said to have lived in a clay tub, eaten raw meat, and masturbated in public to demonstrate his independent nature. Now, if that doesn't scream virtue, what does?

The central theme of Stoic thought is independence from the chaotic nature of society, as well as independence from the chaotic nature of our raw, untamed human experience. The more independent you are, the clearer you think, and therefore the freer you are to live rationally and help others in need. Considering all persons to be manifestations of the universal spirit, Stoics place a great emphasis on readily helping those in need. There is a strong similarity between Stoic principles and Buddhist principles, most importantly the idea that all suffering is a product of desire.

CHAPTER 7

St. Augustine's Highway to Heaven

In the second century A.D., the Romans became aware of a new religion growing in the heart of their empire. It had originated in the Middle East, but it spread, especially among the poor and urban classes: Christianity. Despite its followers being persecuted by emperors like Nero and Diocletian, Christianity continued to expand until, in the reign of Constantine (272–337), it became the official Roman state religion.

In an effort to keep up ratings and avoid controversy, television hasn't talked a lot about religion (I'm talking here about sitcoms and dramas, not the televangelists you can catch on Sunday morning begging for money). Nonetheless, we can still use television to understand some things about the religious philosophy of the early Christian Fathers.

ST. AUGUSTINE

Let's start with Augustine of Hippo (354–430). He became a leader of the church at a very bad time for the Roman Empire. In 410 the Goths, a barbarian tribe, sacked Rome. This event is generally taken by historians as marking the end of the Roman Empire, even though parts of the empire continued and even thrived as late as the fourteenth century. In the fifth century, various tribes that had existed for centuries on the fringes of the empire were now on the move and began to cross the boundaries. The Roman army was no longer able to keep them out, and the empire withdrew troops from the farthest reaches of the empire to defend its center. By the sixth century, for instance, Romans had withdrawn from the province of Britain, leaving the native Romano-Britons to the mercy of invading tribes like the Angles and Saxons.

Meanwhile, in the center of the empire, Christians such as Augustine struggled to understand these events. We know a lot about Augustine because he wrote an autobiography—one of the first people to do so. It's called *The Confessions*, and it's his explanation of how he came to be a Christian.

Augustine started life as a pagan, steeped in Classical philosophy and literature. He lived a hedonistic lifestyle, pretty much the Charlie Harper of his day. He drank, gambled, and slept with women, which resulted in an illegitimate son.

Finally, in Milan, under the influence of his mother and his continuing studies in philosophy, he began to move toward Christianity, though the process took some time. As he famously prayed, "Lord, make me good . . . but not yet." In 386 he converted to Christianity. He lived for a time in a monastic foundation before becoming bishop of Hippo. Even as a Christian, though, he understood the attractions of Classical thought and the non-Christian lifestyle. This is a feature that makes him one of the more interesting and attractive Christian Fathers. Late in life he wrote his most famous work, *The City of God*, which was a bestseller for much of the Middle Ages and into the Renaissance.

In some respects, Augustine after his conversion to Christianity resembles Jonathan Smith, the character played by Michael Landon in *Highway to Heaven*. Smith is an angel, sent to Earth to earn his wings (like Clarence, the angel in *It's a Wonderful Life*; however, it takes Smith a lot longer to earn them—evidently the rules for becoming a fully fledged angel got harder between 1946 when Frank Capra made *It's a Wonderful Life* and the 1980s, when the studio was filming *Highway to Heaven*).

Smith is accompanied by a human, Mark Gordon (Victor French), an ex-policeman. Gordon starts the show as a cynic and largely a nonbeliever—a bit like Augustine in his pre-Christian phase. Even later, when he accepts Smith's angelhood, he has a certain flip way of referring to it.

> **"My name's Gordon. I carry a badge.
> His name's Smith. He carries a harp."**
> —Mark Gordon, *Highway to Heaven*

Even as an angel Smith is occasionally subject to temptation. In an episode titled "One Winged Angels," for example, he falls in love with a woman even though he's supposed to make sure she winds up engaged to someone else.

Touched by an Angel

Highway to Heaven was sufficiently successful that in 1994 CBS launched another show with the same general premise. *Touched by an Angel* starred Roma Downey and Della Reese as angels (Downey was a trainee and Reese was her supervisor) who travel through America bringing God's love and counsel to those in need. The show was produced and largely written by Martha Williamson, a powerful Christian figure in the Hollywood community.

A good deal of the writing for *Touched* sounds as if it could have come straight out of St. Augustine's mouth:

> "We feel we have so much to lose in this world. But then you realize if God is there for you, there really isn't that much to lose."

> "You've had setbacks, and you'll have others. It's not important how many times you've fallen. It's how many times you let God pick you up that matters."

> "How can you judge something fairly when you don't know what the rules are? You can't play God because you aren't God."

All of these comments are similar to what Augustine says both in *The Confessions* and most especially in *The City of God*. Confronting a congregation that wanted to know why their world was collapsing around them, he told them that it wasn't for them to question the judgment of God.

Maybe Della Reese *was* St. Augustine—only black and female.

THE CITY OF GOD MEETS GLEE

Augustine wrote his greatest work when he was older. *The City of God* was his attempt to explain the sack of Rome by the Goths, and it rambles on for twenty-two books, wandering around all sorts of questions such as whether the nuns who were raped in the sack of the city could still be considered virgins (his answer, if you're interested, is yes).

At the heart of the book is the idea of two cities—the Earthly City and the Heavenly City. They're counterposed to one another, and although it was necessary to pass through the Earthly City to attain the Heavenly City, the elect are now part of God's city and are separated from the unbelievers.

To understand this better, think about *Glee* (broadcast on Fox) and the character of Finn, played by Cory Monteith. He started out as a member of the football team—not just any member but the starting quarterback. In the pilot episode of the show, he joined the Glee Club and subjected himself to ridicule and physical harassment by his fellow team members.

HIGH SCHOOL STUDENTS ARE GETTING OLDER AND OLDER THESE DAYS
Cory Monteith and Lea Michele, who plays Rachel on *Glee*, his sometime love interest on the show, may be playing high school students, but they both left school quite a while ago. Monteith was born in 1982, while Michele was born in 1986. However, they're doing better than Tom Welling, who was born in 1977 and is still playing Clark I-just-graduated-from-high-school Kent in *Smallville*.

Finn, in other words, is rather like Augustine. The bishop of Hippo, when young, used to hang out with all the cool pagans, kicking back and reading Classical authors, hitting the best parties in hot spots like Carthage, Milan, and Rome. Then, like Finn, he discovered he was interested in something else—in his case, Christianity; in the case of Finn, music.

Finn understands the sacrifices that he's had to make in joining the Glee Club to hang out with all the misfits and weirdos (though it must be stated that a lot of the female weirdos in Glee Club are really hot; hell, we'd have joined Glee Club in a minute in high school if anyone in it had looked like Lea Michele).

Finn finds that despite the hostility of other students, by sticking together the glee students become stronger. They are the elect, welcomed into the City (or Glee Club) of God. Outside, the barbarians in the form of Cheerios coach Sue Sylvester (Jane Lynch) are waiting to destroy them.

"I wanna pit these kids against one another, am I clear? I am going to create an environment that is so toxic, no one will want to be a part of that club. Like the time I sold my house to a nice young couple, and I salted the earth in the backyard so that nothing living could grow there for a hundred years. You know why I did that? Because they tried to get me to pay their closing costs."
—Sue Sylvester

Just as the Visigoths, the Vandals, and the Ostrogoths raged through the western Roman Empire, carrying off what they could and destroying what they couldn't, so Sue Sylvester wants to raze the Glee

Club at McKinley High down to its foundations. She has no compunction about playing dirty. "You think this is hard?" she snarls to her cheerleaders. "Try being waterboarded! That's hard!"

But just as Augustine claimed that the City of God could never be destroyed by the barbarian hordes because it was immortal, so Will Schuester (Matthew Morrison), Spanish teacher turned leader of the Glee Club, brings his band of misfits through every disaster that Sue throws at them.

> **"Glee club. Every time I try to destroy that clutch of scab-eating mouth breathers it only comes back stronger like some sexually ambiguous horror movie villain. Here I am, about to turn thirty, and I've sacrificed everything only to be shanghaied by the bi-curious machinations of a kabal of doughy, misshapen teens. Am I missing something? Is it me? Of course it's not me. It's Will Schuester."**
>
> —Sue Sylvester

FAITH AND REASON IN THE BUNKER HOUSEHOLD

Mike Stivic: You know, you are totally incomprehensible.

Archie Bunker: Maybe so, but I make a lot of sense.

—All in the Family

"Understanding," says Augustine, "is the reward of faith. Therefore, seek not to understand that you may believe, but believe that you may understand." In other words, first you must believe in something and then, once your faith is strong enough, you find the rational foundations of your faith.

This is pretty much the way Archie Bunker approached life. He was completely confirmed in his opinions and expressed them loudly and at length to anyone who'd listen. Mostly this was his long-suffering son-in-law, Mike Stivic (Rob Reiner), his daughter, Gloria (Sally Struthers), and of course his saintly wife, Edith (Jean Stapleton).

Archie had the greatest contempt for anything that fell outside his experience.

Mike: Why couldn't they say "Buddha, bless you" in Chinese?

Archie: Because they don't say that, that's why. If they say . . . . Well, if they say anything at all, it's "Sayonara."

Mike: That's Japanese.

Archie: Same thing.

Mike: It's not the same thing!

Archie: What are you talking about? You put a Jap and a Chink together, you gonna tell me which is which?

Mike: That's right, because I find out about them. I talk to them as individuals.

Archie: Sure, you talk to them. You say, "Which one of you guys is the Chink?"

Clearly, logic is no good in such circumstances. Poor Mike attacks the ramparts of Archie's bigotry over and over only to fall back, bloody and defeated. Archie starts from belief. Reason comes later, if at all.

Augustine would have understood this. (Well, not the bigotry, perhaps, since he came from north Africa.)

Archie's view of the Christian religion is entirely faith-based. "He made us all one true religion, Edith," he says, "which he named after his son, Christian—or Christ, for short." Augustine and Archie also tend to see eye to eye in the area of ecclesiastical authority. Augustine sees authority as the road to faith:

> "Authority demands belief and prepares man for reason. Reason leads to understanding and knowledge. But reason is not entirely absent from authority, for we have got to consider whom we have to believe."
> —St. Augustine

Archie has faith in his own authority and, to some degree, in that of his minister. But like Augustine, he rejects authority that is not backed by reason. Speaking of the pope, he says:

> "I ain't got no respect for no religion where the head guy claims he can't make no mistakes. Like he's, waddya call, inflammable."

CHAPTER 8
Scully Shaves Mulder with Ockham's Razor

With the final collapse of the western Roman Empire in the fifth century, Europe entered a long period that historians call the Middle Ages. They used to call it the Dark Ages, but then someone pointed out that during the twelfth and thirteenth centuries some great universities were founded (Paris, Bologna, Modena, Oxford, Cambridge), some great art was produced, and generally things didn't seem so very dark.

Now historians just call the first part of the Middle Ages dark—roughly from about A.D. 600 to 1000. During that time, the Catholic Church was one of the few stable institutions. People lived out their lives without knowing how to read or write, in complete ignorance, for the most part, of all the learning that had come down from the Greeks and Romans.

GREEK BY WAY OF ISLAM

While Europe was sunk in the darkness of the early medieval period, a new force arose in the East: Islam. Founded by the Prophet Mohammed in the seventh century, Islam spread rapidly, conquering the Middle East, northern Africa, Spain, and much of Eastern Europe. Islamic scholars were fascinated by the philosophical writings of the Greeks, especially Aristotle. They translated many of Aristotle's writings into Arabic. Later, when learning began to revive in Europe, scholars retranslated Aristotle from Arabic into Latin so he could be read at the European universities. We have Islam and the Arabs to thank for the preservation and transmission of this part of Greece's philosophic heritage.

FAITH, REASON, AND *THE X-FILES*

By the onset of the High Middle Ages, a lot of philosophic debate revolved around the problem of the relationship between faith and reason. Remember, this was the issue that Augustine tried to resolve in the fifth century and that preoccupied Archie Bunker in the twentieth century. But philosophers in the eleventh and twelfth centuries continued to chew on it.

One of the reasons this was so interesting to them was that in the twelfth century the writings of Aristotle on logic were trickling into Europe. Scholars wanted to take this shiny new logical method and apply it to what they were most familiar with: the doctrines of Christianity and the Church.

Aquinas and the *Summa Theologiae*

The most obsessive about this project was Thomas Aquinas (later made a saint by the church). Aquinas (1225–1274) lived in Italy (or rather, what we now call Italy). He was a large man, very slow and quiet. His schoolmates called him "Dumb Ox." He joined the Dominican order of monks, much against the wishes of his family. They sent a beautiful woman to his room one night to persuade him to abandon his vows, but Thomas drove her away with a lighted brand snatched from the hearth. He must have been a barrel of laughs at parties.

> **"Happiness is secured through virtue; it is a good attained by man's own will."**
> —Aquinas

Aquinas decided to apply his logic in a searching examination of the whole of Christian doctrine. The result was two works: the *Summa contra Gentiles* and the *Summa Theologiae*. The latter, unfinished at the time of Aquinas's death, ran to five fun-packed volumes and is practically unreadable, even though it's officially part of Catholic doctrine.

In the *Summa Theologiae*, Aquinas takes each point of Christian dogma, offers several objections to it, and then applies Aristotelian logic to show how each of these objections can be overcome. It's sort of what would happen if Mr. Spock were suddenly to become a Christian and begin proselytizing aboard the Starship *Enterprise*.

Aquinas believes that God is the prime mover of the universe, the force that controls everyone's actions. This, of course, raises the problem of free will. If God controls our actions, how could, for instance, Beaver Cleaver keep getting into trouble and have to be straightened out by Ward or June (with the occasional help of Wally)?

Aquinas has an answer for this. God, he says, doesn't make Beaver do everything necessarily; He causes Beaver to act contingently.

> **"A man has free choice to the extent that he is rational."**
> —Aquinas

Beaver Cleaver and Free Will

This is kind of a confusing idea, but here's what Aquinas is getting at:

Ward helps the Beav and Wally build a racing car out of scraps of wood and a single-cylinder motor (Ward is the kind of nauseatingly wholesome father who helps his kids do stuff like that). He warns them not to be careless or reckless with it. In this sense, he's like God, giving them the wherewithal to have fun and enjoy life but placing limitations on their ability to do so. Notice that he doesn't do anything that would actually *prevent* them from being careless with the racing car—he just imposes a moral imperative not to.

The Beaver, egged on by his best friend Larry Mondello, drives the race car onto the street, where he's promptly pulled over by a policeman.

This is an example of Beaver acting contingently; he knows what he should do, but he has the free will to do something else if he chooses. In a world without free will, he wouldn't be able to do anything but act responsibly. This being the world of Aquinas's God, he listens to bad advice and defies God's (or, if you like, Ward's) instructions.

To prevent Ward from finding out what's happened, Wally agrees that when Beaver appears in court he'll pretend to be the Beav's guardian. The judge calls up both boys, lectures them until Beaver starts bawling, and tells them it's up to them whether they tell their parents what they did. Both boys confess to Ward, and he tells them it doesn't matter what sort of trouble they get into; they can always come to him. God, in other words, loves a sinner no matter what.

June: Beaver, I just hope you realize that wherever you go or whatever you do, there's always somebody watching you.

Beaver: Sure, Mom. You watch me, Dad watches me, when I'm at school the teacher watches me, and when I go to the movies, the ushers watch me.

June: No, Beaver, I mean somebody else.

Beaver: Gee, Mom, do you mean like, God?

June: Mmm-hmmmm, and if you do something bad you're going to hurt Him.

Beaver: I would want to do anything to hurt God. He's got enough trouble with the Russians and all.

Aquinas's explanation of the relationship between God's imperatives and free will comforted generations of Catholics and continues to do so to this day. We choose the greatest happiness, he says, by doing that which is pleasing to God. The Beaver would have been happier if he'd ignored Larry, listened to Ward, and stayed on the sidewalk. But because our human nature is corrupted by original sin (a concept left over from Augustine's interpretation of Christianity), humans tend to stray off the sidewalk of life and into the street, where they have to periodically get smacked down by policemen and judges.

WILLIAM OF OCKHAM: THE TRUTH ISN'T "OUT THERE"

Aquinas's philosophical school has become known as Scholasticism. Like the culture of the High Middle Ages, it was extremely intellectual, orderly, and rigid in its application. William of Ockham (1290–1349) is in every way a more attractive figure.

Ockham was a Franciscan—that is, he belonged to the monastic order founded by St. Francis of Assisi. He studied at the universities of Oxford and Paris and had a relatively uneventful academic career until 1324, when he was accused of heresy. The church at the time was involved in a nasty political controversy (during which time, for about seventy years, the spiritual capital of Christianity was moved from Rome to the French city of Avignon), and the Franciscan order was caught up in the middle of it. William became involved with the medieval prince Louis of Bavaria, who had denounced the papacy. William lived at Louis's court until 1347, when Louis died. William himself died two years later, probably of the Black Death, which killed almost a third of the population of Europe in the fourteenth century.

Ockham's philosophical approach has been called Skepticism—it was certainly skeptical of Aquinas and most of Scholasticism. In his *Sententiae* and *Quodlibeta*, Ockham questioned everything and anything. Aquinas believed in trying to reconcile Faith and Reason; Ockham rejected this project. Faith is Faith, he maintained, and Reason is Reason. You can't use one to prove or support the other. Ockham argued that we know and can understand the physical world. Faith, however, deals with the unseen and therefore the unknowable. To understand this viewpoint, let's turn to one of the most innovative shows of the 1990s: *The X-Files*.

Fox Mulder: The Anti-Ockhamite

In 1993 the Fox network began airing *The X-Files*. The show almost immediately became a cult hit and lasted until 2002. The premise of the show was a partnership between two FBI agents, Fox Mulder (David Duchovny) and Dana Scully (Gillian Anderson), as they investigated reports of alien sightings, paranormal experiences, and other cases at the fringe of reality. (The show *Fringe*, which Fox began showing in fall 2008, is based on a somewhat similar premise, though with some significant differences.)

Mulder: Sorry, nobody down here but the FBI's most unwanted.

Scully: Agent Mulder? I'm Dana Scully. I've been assigned to work with you.

Mulder: Oh, isn't it nice to be suddenly so highly regarded. So, who did you tick off to get stuck with this detail, Scully?

Scully: Actually, I'm looking forward to working with you. I've heard a lot about you.

Mulder: Oh, really? I was under the impression that you were sent to spy on me.

Of the two agents, Scully is the skeptic. She's not willing to believe in anything unless there's clear, physical evidence. This stance became somewhat ridiculous as the show continued; by the time the show was in its fourth or fifth season, Mulder and Scully had encountered enough aliens to populate a couple of planets, yet Scully still acted surprised every time they ran into one. You'd think she'd have learned.

Mulder, on the other hand, is a believer. In his grimy office, he has scores of books, files, and reports of every crackpot theory in existence.

It seems as if he gives all of them the same degree of credence. This includes not only accounts of aliens landing on Earth and strange creatures inhabiting swamps outside New Orleans; it also encompasses government conspiracies, everything from the assassination of JFK to Jim Morrison being alive and well and living in Paris. Mulder believes *everything*. In that sense, he embodies Augustine's idea that Faith supports Reason. Aquinas, if you remember, had stood that notion on its head and argued that Reason can support Faith. Ockham takes on Aquinas, Augustine, and Fox Mulder, arguing that Faith and Reason have nothing to do with one another.

The conspiracy that Mulder—and eventually Scully—comes to believe in is one that is vast, reaching the highest echelons of the government, largely presided over by a mysterious figure known as the "Cigarette-Smoking Man."

TV CONSPIRACIES

From 1996 to 2000, NBC aired *The Pretender*, starring Michael T. Weiss as a genius who, as a child, had been kidnapped by and forced to work for a mysterious organization known as "The Centre." As an adult, he broke from the Centre and went rogue. Pursued by an attractive Centre operative, Miss Parker, he uncovered more and more of the Centre's mysterious plot. The decade of the 1990s was a very big time for conspiracy-based TV.

At the end of the series, Mulder and Scully went on the run after Mulder was convicted by a military tribunal of disrupting plans for the alien invasion of Earth. Two movies were made based on the show, after which Duchovny and Anderson both found better things to do with their time and *The X-Files* faded from memory.

Now let's return to William of Ockham. To undermine what he saw as fanciful claims concerning Faith and Reason, he developed the logical tool known as "Ockham's Razor." It's sometimes phrased as "Causes should not be multiplied without necessity."

All this is to say that if we have something for which there are two alternate explanations, the simpler explanation is more likely to be the true one.

For instance, in Scully's viewpoint, John F. Kennedy was assassinated in Dallas, Texas, on November 22, 1963, by a lone gunman, Lee Harvey Oswald, who was later shot by a Dallas nightclub owner, Jack Ruby. Mulder, on the other hand, argues that the assassination was the result of a vast conspiracy, with participants ranging from the military-industrial complex to members of a secret organization (of whom Cigarette-Smoking Man is the representative). All of the parts of this conspiracy had to work in concert with one another to cause the shots to be fired shortly after 12:30 P.M. on November 22, killing Kennedy (though of course, in Mulder's view, it's nonsense to believe that Oswald fired those shots and even more nonsense to think there was a single gunman).

> **"It is futile to do with more things that which can be done with fewer."**
> —William of Ockham

Let's apply Ockham's Razor: Which explanation is simpler? Which has fewer moving parts? And which "multiplies causes without necessity"?

Clearly Ockham would have preferred Scully's no-nonsense theory of the Kennedy assassination.

Their approaches are contrasted throughout the series:

Mulder: You have to be willing to see.

Scully: I wish it were that simple.

Mulder: Scully, you have to believe me. Nobody else on this whole damn planet does or ever will. You're my one in five billion.

Despite Mulder's appeal, Scully remains the skeptic. Her heroes are—or ought to be, anyway—William of Ockham and another medieval scholar, Roger Bacon.

Bacon (1214–1294), like Ockham, was a Franciscan. He was less interested than Ockham in pure philosophy. In today's world, he'd have been a scientist; he was deeply interested in the natural world and believed in the value of observation and experiment. Not surprisingly, it got him into trouble, and he was accused on several occasions of practicing black magic.

> "Reasoning draws a conclusion, but does not make the conclusion certain, unless the mind discovers it by the path of experience."
> —Roger Bacon

It's not enough, in other words, to theorize the existence of aliens or swamp creatures; we have to actually experience them and validate their actuality by means of experiment. This is just what Scully tries to do, despite Mulder's impatience with her reluctance to draw firm conclusions on the basis of evidence that wouldn't convince anyone. "In most of my work," Mulder says, "the laws of physics don't seem to apply." Bacon would find this attitude ridiculous. The laws of physics *always* apply—even in Agent Mulder's universe.

The skepticism of thinkers like Ockham and Bacon mark a sharp break from the conventional wisdom of the preceding Middle Ages. They're less willing to accept things on faith, more demanding in their standards of truth. This isn't to say they aren't deeply religious, merely that they don't content themselves with either the Augustinian idea that Faith supports Reason or Aquinas's notion that the tenets of Faith can be supported and proved by Reason.

By the end of the fourteenth century, Europe was on the brink of a vast new cultural expansion: the Renaissance.

CHAPTER 9
Larry Hagman Dreams of Descartes

"Except our own thoughts, there is nothing absolutely in our power."
—Rene Descartes

Major Nelson: How are things going?

Jeannie: Terrible. I have to make dinner—I mean actually make it without magic. We are liable to die.

To all intents and purposes, modern philosophy starts with René Descartes (1596–1650). Most of the problems that philosophers are still batting back and forth today are ones that Descartes dealt with, although often in different forms. Descartes also lived during the start of the greatest scientific revolution in history, one that's still going on. Think about what happened from the middle of the sixteenth century to the end of the seventeenth:

- **1543:** Nicolaus Copernicus published his theory that the Earth and the other planets went round the Sun, instead of the Earth sitting at the center of the universe.
- **1564:** Galileo Galilei was born. In his lifetime he provided essential experimental evidence for Copernicus's theory of the solar system.
- **1609:** Johannes Kepler published his laws of planetary motion.
- **1628:** William Harvey published his book on the circulation of the blood.
- **1642:** Blaise Pascal invented the mechanical calculator.
- **1643:** Isaac Newton was born. He developed the theory of gravity, which is the basis of all modern physics.
- **1675:** Gottfried Wilhelm Leibniz invented differential calculus.

And these are just the highlights. Pretty much the whole foundation of modern science was created during these years.

It was also a period of religious wars throughout much of Europe. Descartes, who was born in the French province of Touraine, tried to stay away from the fighting and find peace and quiet so that he could work on his philosophic and mathematical ideas. After 1626 he settled in Paris, where he tried to sleep until noon every day. Friends persisted in waking him earlier than he wanted to get out of bed, and to get away from them he finally fled to Holland, where he settled for most of the rest of his life. He died in Sweden after a correspondence with the queen of Sweden led him to move to that country as a kind of royal in-house philosopher.

EARLY TO RISE MAKES A MAN DEAD

Queen Christina of Sweden was accustomed to begin the business of her court very early in the morning. The only time during the day she could regularly spare to talk to Descartes was at 5 A.M. He tried to accommodate her, but this early rising, combined with the cold of the Scandinavian winter, caused him to fall ill and die. So much for Franklin's old line about "Early to bed, early to rise."

DESCARTES'S PHILOSOPHY

Descartes approached the problem of how to create a basis for his philosophy by what came to be called Cartesian Doubt. He begins by deciding to doubt everything that he possibly can. Is he sitting in his house? Maybe, but his senses might be mistaken. Is it raining outside? Again, the rain and cold could be an illusion. Is the fire burning? Possibly not—maybe he's only imagining it.

He continues this line of thought until he comes to the most basic question of all: Is he thinking? To this, he answers yes, I must be thinking, because if I weren't, I couldn't think about thinking. So he formulates his famous statement: *Cogito ergo sum.* I think, therefore I am.

But, continues Descartes, if God is perfect—and one can't conceive of a God who isn't—he wouldn't deceive man by deliberately fooling his senses. There must be more to it than this. Descartes's solution is to distinguish between subjective experience (what he calls *res cogitans*, a fancy Latin term for something that exists purely as thought) and external experience—that is, things that exist apart from us. Looked at another way, Descartes is saying that the universe consists of him and everything else. The philosophic term for this division is *Cartesian Dualism.*

To understand a bit better how this idea of starting from one's own existence works, let's consider *I Dream of Jeannie.* This might seem an odd starting point, but after all, one of the big questions in the show was whether Larry Hagman was just imagining all the strange things that kept happening when he was around Jeannie. He knew he wasn't, but others weren't so sure.

Starring Barbara Eden and Larry Hagman, the show first aired in 1965 and ran until 1970. The premise was simple: Major Tony Nelson, an astronaut, is briefly stranded on a desert island after a space shot. While there, he frees a beautiful genie from her bottle, and she immediately attaches herself to him as her new master.

We know what you're thinking: Most of us should have such a problem, right? But since this was 1960s television, everyone was inhibited and uptight (it was the Nixon administration, for God's sake!). And Tony spent most of his time persuading his superiors and especially the army psychologist Colonel Alfred E. Bellows (Hayden Rorke), that Jeannie wasn't anything more than a very attractive, ordinary girl.

HORRORS! A NAVEL!
Believe it or not, in its day *I Dream of Jeannie* was considered daring. First, Jeannie lived with Tony Nelson, to whom she wasn't married. Second, Barbara Eden almost always appeared in her "Jeannie" outfit, consisting of harem pants, a bare midriff, and a vest and blouse. Network executives got around the censors on the first issue by pointing out that Jeannie slept in a bottle and not in Tony's bed. On the second issue, they had to agree never to show Barbara Eden's navel during the show.

Here's an exchange from the show's pilot.

Col. Alfred E. Bellows, MD: What was this genie like?

Major Nelson: Oh, she was—um, just your average, everyday, run-of-the-mill genie.

Bellows: Of course. Beautiful?

Nelson: Yes, yeah.

Bellows: Desirable? And helpful?

Nelson: Yes, yes.

Bellows: Captain, that's the classic fantasy. A beautiful girl on a desert island. A girl who would do anything for you. Do you know who that girl was?

Nelson: No, sir. I've never seen her before in my life.

Bellows: She was your mother.

Nelson: My mother's in Salt Lake City, sir.

Bellows: I'm a psychiatrist. I know a mother when I see one.

Colonel Bellows is the Cartesian philosopher, resolved to doubt everything he can. Tony Nelson is willing to believe the evidence of his senses, but Col. Bellows knows better. Senses can be wrong. The deeper truth is that Jeannie represents Tony's mother, even if Tony himself is unaware of the fact.

In *Discourse on Method* and *Meditations*, the two works that set out his philosophic theories in some detail, Descartes discusses the possibility that what he sees—or rather, what he thinks he sees—may be the result of a hallucination. His only hope is to return to his sense of self, his awareness of his own existence through the medium of his thoughts.

"While I wanted to think everything false, it must necessarily be that I who thought was something; and remarking that this truth, *I think, therefore I am*, was so solid and so certain that all the most extravagant suppositions of the skeptics were incapable of upsetting it, I judged that I could receive it without scruple as the first principle of the philosophy that I sought."
—Descartes

A similar problem was encountered by Darrin Stephens, the husband in *Bewitched*. The show ran 1964–1972, more or less the same period as *I Dream of Jeannie*, and covered the same ground. Samantha (Elizabeth Montgomery), a witch, falls in love with Darrin (Dick York/Dick Sargent), and marries him. Darrin then has to come to terms with her powers, which he does mainly by telling her not to use them. You and we have already figured out that Darrin's one of the biggest pricks in the universe, but Samantha, against all the odds, loves him and stays married to him—God knows why.

In the same way that Tony Nelson had to gradually revolt against his Cartesian grounding and learn to trust his senses over his intellect, Darrin has to accept that there are more things in heaven and on earth than are thought of in his philosophy.

Darrin: You're a what?

Samantha: I'm a witch.

Darrin: That's wonderful. We'll talk about it tomorrow.

Samantha: Now. I am a witch. A real house-haunting, broom-riding, cauldron-stirring witch.

Eventually, once he gets over the shock, Darrin agrees that Samantha is a witch. We can't imagine Descartes, if he ever formed a liaison with a witch, making the same concession.

Bobby in the Shower

The issue of whether our senses can deceive us was played out to the greatest absurdity midway through the prime-time soap *Dallas*. It seems hard to believe today, but at one point shows like *Dallas*, *Dynasty*, and *Falcon Crest* dominated evening viewing. *Dallas* revolved around two brothers: J. R. Ewing (Larry Hagman), the evil, amoral brother; and Bobby Ewing (Patrick Duffy), the good, caring, moral brother.

Around the sixth season, Duffy indicated he had other projects and didn't want to come back. The writers obligingly killed off his character (he was run over by a car, driven by his sister-in-law), after which his poor grieving widow, Pam (Victoria Principal), settled down to rebuild her life.

Duffy soon discovered that life after *Dallas* had its challenges, the main one of which was that no one wanted to hire him for anything else. He said he'd be willing to come back to the show, and the writers, suppressing a natural desire to dip him slowly in boiling oil and watch him squirm, did some more rewriting. Midway through the 1986 season Pam woke up, heard someone in the bathroom, and found Bobby calmly showering. She realized that the entire 1984–85 season had been nothing but a dream sequence, and *Dallas* settled down to another five years of overacting, stupid plot twists, and ghastly writing.

Bobby might well have said to himself, "I shower, therefore I am."

THE MEASURE OF A MAN

As we saw earlier, Descartes made a distinction between things of the mind and things that are external to us (remember, this is called Cartesian Dualism). Things outside of us, he said, are governed by the laws of mathematics, which can be discovered by human reason. This was a pretty amazing assertion, since it said that science rather than Faith alone was capable of understanding the universe. But this was also a natural outgrowth of the age of science in which Descartes was living.

> **"The laws of mechanics are identical with those of nature."**
> —Descartes

The logic of this approach led Descartes to think of the bodies of humans and animals as machines, obeying the laws of mechanics. Humans, unlike animals, have souls (which reside, for some reason, in the pineal gland), but our bodies work exactly like machines. Which naturally raises the question: What defines a soul?

It so happens that this issue came up in *Star Trek: The Next Generation* in an episode titled "The Measure of a Man." The episode is concerned with Lt. Commander Data, an android, who is a member of the crew aboard the Starship *Enterprise*. Commander Bruce Maddox comes aboard the *Enterprise* to inform Captain Picard that he intends to take Data back to Earth and disassemble him to find out how he works. When Picard and Data object, Maddox informs them that Starfleet doesn't consider Data a person and therefore he has no say in the matter.

What Makes a Person?

The term *person* is derived from the Latin *persona*, meaning "mask." Philosophers have long debated the criteria for determining personhood. Broadly defined, a person is any individual self-conscious or rational being. More narrowly, a person is defined as an individual human being. Descartes, as we've seen, defines humans as beings in possession of souls.

The question that Maddox, Picard, and Data grapple with is: What does it take to be a person? Can a nonhuman agent be a person if it is capable of the same high-level cognitive functions? What else do you need to be able to do or think or feel in order to gain inclusion into this exclusive club?

Descartes starts from the standpoint that our bodies are mere machines. In this respect, Data isn't different from any other member of the *Enterprise* crew, or, for that matter, from Commander Maddox. The distinction is that Maddox and Picard have a certain, indefinable "something" that sets them apart.

A hearing is set to determine Data's personhood. The presiding judge advocate, Phillipa Louvois, orders Commander Riker to serve as prosecutor, while Picard volunteers to defend Data's rights as a person. Riker, a good Cartesian, shows that Data is so much a machine that he can actually be turned off. This seems to clinch the matter; Data, in the words of Louvois, "is a toaster."

Not so fast, counters Picard. He challenges Maddox directly. What are the qualifications for personhood?

Maddox replies that the three qualifications are:

- Intelligence
- Self-awareness
- Consciousness

Maddox insists that Data, despite being intelligent—which he defines as the ability to "cope with new information"—is not a person because he fails to meet two additional requirements for personhood: self-awareness and consciousness. Picard challenges this thesis.

Picard: What about self-awareness? What does that mean? Why am I self-aware?

Maddox: Because you are conscious of your existence and actions. You are aware of your self and your own ego.

Picard: Commander Data. What are you doing now?

Data: I am taking part in a legal hearing to determine my rights and status. Am I a person or am I property?

Picard: And what is at stake?

Data: My right to choose. Perhaps my very life.

Picard: "My rights" . . . "my status" . . . "my right to choose" . . . "my life." He seems reasonably self-aware to me.

The hearing turns on the issue of whether, as Louvois says, Data has a soul. In other words, it depends precisely on the issue Descartes identified as the criterion for personhood. In a final burst of righteous anger, Picard declares:

> **"Your honor, a courtroom is a crucible. In it we burn away the egos, the selfish desires, the half-truths, until we're left with the pure product—a truth—for all time. Sooner or later it's going to happen. This man or others like him are going to succeed in replicating Data. And then we have to decide—what are they? And how will we treat these creations of our genius? The decision you reach here today stretches far beyond this android and this courtroom. It will reveal the kind of a people we are. And what [points to Data] they are going to be. Do you condemn them to slavery? Starfleet was founded to seek out new life. Well, there he sits, your honor, waiting on our decision."**

The episode ends with the court deciding in favor of Data. He may be a machine, but he is one with a soul. Cartesianism has triumphed in the twenty-fourth century.

CHAPTER 10

Locke versus Hobbes, or The Brady Bunch Takes on Survivor

If you remember anything from your high school history classes, you'll know that the seventeenth and eighteenth centuries were a time of political turmoil. The old monarchies in Europe were beginning to crumble. Louis XIV of France, one of the most powerful kings ever, died in 1715. He probably never said, "*L'etat, c'est moi!*" (The state is me), but that was the way his thinking ran. But when he died, Europe had been wracked for years by a series of wars and revolutions that continued on for a century or so after Louis's body was put into the ground.

The big revolutions were the English Revolution, also called the Glorious Revolution, which took place in 1688 and overthrew the monarchy of James II, replacing him with King William and Queen Mary; the American Revolution, which began in 1775 and ended in 1789 with the drawing up of the Constitution; and the French Revolution, which began in 1789 and went on until 1799. When the dust of the French Revolution cleared, the French had overthrown their king, Louis XVI, cut off his head (and that of his wife, Marie Antoinette); tried a U.S.-style republic; and finished off with a military dictatorship/empire led by Napoleon Bonaparte.

Obviously all this gave philosophers a lot to do. It was all very well to overthrow the king and declare that something new had to be put in his place, but that left the question of *what* to replace him with. During the century or so before the American and French revolutions broke out, philosophers had been extremely busy constructing theories of political power, coming up with all sorts of ideas about how societies ought to be structured. Among the most important of these philosophers was John Locke.

THE KEY TO LOCKE

Locke (1632–1704) was an Englishman, although Americans such as Thomas Jefferson used his theories as the basis for rebelling against the rule of Britain over the American colonies. Reason plays a big role in his philosophy. Like Roger Bacon, he generally thinks that our knowledge comes through experience. This makes him, in philosophic terms, an empiricist. He wrote his two *Treatises on Government* right after the Glorious Revolution of 1688. Locke starts by arguing that political power isn't hereditary. He says that humans are born into a "state of nature" and that in this state they're governed by "nature's law."

Government is necessary because Natural Law is inadequate for humans who want to exist in happiness. One school of thought in the eighteenth century said that governments derived power and authority from God. Certain people (i.e., kings) were designated by God to rule everyone else.

Locke rejects that idea and says that government is essentially a contract that's established between people who agree to be governed by its rules. (The French philosopher Jean-Jacques Rousseau wrote a whole book about this, titled *The Social Contract*.)

Marcia Brady Explains John Locke

Think for a minute about *The Brady Bunch*. We know, we know. Once you start, you can't get the goddamn words out of your head. Smack yourself a couple of times to get rid of the tune and bear with us. Ready?

The Brady Bunch is a reasonably good example of a social contract at work.

The show ran from 1969 to 1974 and starred Florence Henderson as Carol Brady, Robert Reed as Mike Brady, and an adorable (vomit in mouth) bunch of kids played by Barry Williams (Greg), Maureen McCormick (Marcia), Christopher Knight (Peter), Eve Plumb (Jan), Mike Lookinland (Bobby), and Susan Olsen (Cindy). The Bradys are, in today's parlance, a "blended" family—Mike had the boys from a previous marriage, while Carol was bringing up the girls on her own.

It was the sort of setup that sitcoms in the 1960s loved—a chance to follow the wacky but lovable antics of a bunch of cute kids and their loving and all-wise parents. The conflicts were, as you might expect, mainly between the boys and the girls.

Consider the following situation, typical of the show, in which Marcia has lost her diary and accused one of the boys of taking it.

Marcia: Okay, if you hand it right over, I won't press charges.

Greg: What are you talking about?

Marcia: As if you didn't know.

Peter: Bobby, do you know what she's talking about?

Bobby: No. Greg, do you know what she's talking about?

Greg: No. Marcia, do you know what you're talking about?

Marcia: I certainly do, someone in this room took my diary.

Greg: Your diary, you mean you actually keep one of those stupid things?

Bobby: What's a diary?

Peter: It's a book that you write things that you don't want anyone else to know.

Bobby: Why?

Greg: So, you could write stuff like [sits at his desk imitating Marcia writing in her diary] "Dear diary, at last I met him, my dream man, it was at the delicatessen and our fingers tingled as we reached over for the same potato salad."

Marcia: I have never written any ridiculous thing like that in my diary!

Peter: You didn't?

Marcia: I should say not!

Greg: Then, why are you afraid that somebody might read it?

Marcia: None of your business.

Just makes you want to bust a gut laughing, doesn't it? Well, maybe not.

The point here is that Carol and Mike and their kids have agreed to live in the same household according to certain rules. These were agreed on when Carol and Mike got married, and everyone's obliged to live by them, even if they don't always like the results. In this case, Marcia can appeal to higher authorities (her parents), since the boys have broken the rules by stealing her diary. In the same way, according to Locke, free people in the state of nature come together to form a social compact that binds all of its members.

HOBBES

Locke's contemporary was Thomas Hobbes (1588–1679). Hobbes believed in putting political philosophy on a scientific basis, much as was being done with the natural sciences. In this respect, he's the founder of modern sociology.

Hobbes is much more pessimistic than Locke (to an extent, Locke's arguments can be taken as answers to Hobbes). He believes that the natural state of man is conflict. Men, if not restrained by society, will be perpetually at war with one another.

> **"The life of man, solitary, poor, nasty, brutish, and short."**
> —Thomas Hobbes

In order to prevent them from destroying each other, humans enter into a compact, which Hobbes characterizes as a kind of collective tyranny called *Leviathan*. He identifies three kinds of government—monarchy, democracy, and aristocracy—and says he's firmly in favor of monarchy as the least open to corruption.

Hobbes's society isn't motivated by natural law—a concept he rejected—but by self-interest. Humans obey the laws laid down by Leviathan because they're better off if they do.

In many respects, the world of *Survivor* is the embodiment of Hobbes's state. The individuals who make up the "cast" of the reality show are all striving to win by conquering each other. The show forces them into a compact, however temporary, and enforces rules that prevent them from simply randomly destroying one another. Their struggle for individual victory takes place within this constructed structure. It's a very different world from the sunny, cheerful social contract that runs the Brady household. Hobbes's philosophy would become the basis for what we might think of as enlightened despotism. Locke's much more liberal thinking, on the other hand, became a central element in the construction of the American republic.

Both Carroll O'Connor's Archie Bunker and William Shatner's Ed Goodson on *$h*! My Dad Says* are examples of the Hobbesian hero at work. Both are strongly opinionated, but both know that if only everyone would just do as they say, the world would work fine. They don't try to build up a consensus about anything; their comments have the force of divine decrees. And, like Hobbesian heroes, they sometimes have to choose between being right and being effective.

Bonnie: Ed, do you wanna be right, or you wanna get laid?

Ed: That's right, I've never been both.

On the other hand, Mike Brady was more Lockean. His social contract with Florence Henderson (somehow it seems more fitting to think of it as a social contract than as a marriage, since if we call it a marriage we have to imagine Florence Henderson having sex) was entered into voluntarily and for purposes of giving the children a better place in which to grow up. It's true that they sometimes tried to kill each other, but the Bradys always got through these situations by stressing fair play and mutual interest. This kind of liberal thinking extends to the whole neighborhood in which the Bradys live.

Mike Brady: Our house is more important than money. This neighborhood is more important than money. Tell me. How many times have we borrowed each other's power tools or patched up each other's kids? We know so much about each other. I know that every January, Mr. Yeager is going to have that big Super Bowl party at his house. We know that every spring, Mrs. Simmons is going to have the prettiest daffodils on the block. We know that at 10:15 every Saturday morning, Mrs. Topping likes to walk through her living room naked. Call me old-fashioned, but these things are important, and they're not for sale. This is our neighborhood, and we're staying.

A TALE OF A SOCIAL CONTRACT

Though you'd think that being shipwrecked on a desert island is one situation that would call for stern, uncompromising leadership, *Gilligan's Island* was pretty much based on Locke's ideas. Whenever the islanders had to make some big decision—supplementing their food supply, figuring out how to light a signal fire, deciding where to build a movie studio for Ginger and Mary Ann to prance around in—they talked among themselves until they came to an agreement. Under normal circumstances, with a presumed scarcity of resources they'd all be at each other's throats in a matter of a few days, if not hours. This being television, they exist in a paradise. So think of *Gilligan's Island* as Locke's vision of society, and take *Survivor* as an idea of what Hobbes thought humans are like.

Locke is also big on tolerance, which he says is necessary because different people have different abilities, and just as children in the same family can grow up to be different, so different members of society come together to make it a whole.

Sounds like a Very Brady idea.

The West Wing

Although television in the United States never shied away from war-based shows (*Combat, Rat Patrol,* and *Convoy,* to name a few), for some reason it stayed entirely away from America's own Civil War and almost entirely away from the American Revolutionary War. (There was briefly, in 1970, a show called *The Young Rebels,* set in 1777 and concerned with a group of young people fighting the British. Its stars were Richard Ely, Alex Henteloff, Hilary Thompson, and, believe it or not, Lou Gossett Jr. as an escaped slave. If you blinked, you missed it.) As well, for a long time television was reluctant to make political shows, evidently feeling that there was too great a chance of alienating whichever part of its audience didn't like the policies of the politicians being depicted.

The West Wing was the most successful show to get away from this state of mind. Running from 1999 to 2006, it starred Martin Sheen as President Josiah Bartlet and had an ensemble cast that at various points included Rob Lowe, Allison Janney, Alan Alda, Kristin Chenoweth, Dulé Hill, and Jimmy Smits.

The series purported to show the inner life of the White House, framed through the eyes of mid- to high-level staffers and advisors in a liberal presidential administration. Sheen's Bartlet was a largely sympathetic character, though from time to time he had moments of moral collywobbles.

The West Wing was a demonstration of how Locke's social contract works at its best. It was how you wished the president and his aides would really behave in moments of crisis. It depicted complex people, including those of substantially different political persuasions, living and working in harmony toward a common goal—the betterment of the American people. As someone said, "It's about intelligent people having intelligent conversations."

Bartlet: C. J., on your tombstone it's gonna read "Post hoc ergo propter hoc."

C. J.: Okay, but none of my visitors are going to be able to understand my tombstone.

Bartlet: Twenty-seven lawyers in the room, anybody know "post hoc, ergo propter hoc"? Josh?

Josh: Ah, post, after hoc, ergo, therefore . . . . After hoc, therefore something else hoc.

Bartlet: Thank you. Next? Leo.

Leo: "After it, therefore because of it."

Bartlet: "After it, therefore because of it." It means one thing follows the other, therefore it was caused by the other. But it's not always true. In fact it's hardly ever true. We did not lose Texas because of the hat joke. Do you know when we lost Texas?

C. J.: When you learned to speak Latin?

Bartlet: Go figure.

Writer Aaron Sorkin's depiction of an idealistic and committed staff could get out of hand at times. One television critic queried caustically, "What rock did these morally pure creatures crawl out from under?" But for the most part, the writing by Sorkin, the show's creator, strove for some degree of realism.

This included, from time to time, flashes of Hobbesian nastiness. At one point during season four, Bartlet ordered the covert assassination of the Qumar Defence Minister and had several discussions with his chief of staff and others about how to cover up U.S. involvement in the killing. Hobbes would have completely understood this, while lamenting the weakness that makes Bartlet's position as president contingent on the will of the people to elect him. This sort of Lockean system of checks and balances constantly frustrates the Hobbes-inspired characters on the show. Consider the following, in which Leo McGarry, Bartlet's chief of staff, is talking to Admiral Percy Fitzwallace, chairman of the Joint Chiefs of Staff, and Dr. Nancy McNally, National Security Advisor, about what action to take against the rogue Middle Eastern state of Qumar.

McNally: Let's attack.

Fitzwallace: Who?

McNally: Qumar. Let's recommend to the President that we attack.

Leo: Why?

McNally: 'Cause I've had it.

Fitzwallace: I don't think the UN is going to let us do it for that reason.

McNally: That's 'cause you're a sissy. You want peace in the Middle East? Give me a pair of third generation ICBMs and a compass. You get B-2 Spirit stealth bombers over Qumar right now as if the Qumari Air Defense System requires stealth capability. Just fly in at night, and while you're at it, could you order the USS *Louisiana* to fire off a D-5 Trident just to see if it works? What's the worst that could happen?

Fitzwallace: [to Leo, bewildered] Is she talking to me?

McNally: Yes!

Fitzwallace: Well, 98 percent of all living organisms within a seven-mile radius would die instantly in a torrent of fire.

McNally: Admiral Sissymary . . . . We're running out of options on the menu.

If the United States had built its constitution on the foundations laid by Thomas Hobbes instead of John Locke, President Bartlet might well have ordered a nuclear strike against Qumar. As it is, he didn't, and we can all breathe a little easier.

CHAPTER 11

Can or Can't Kant
Like Vampires?

Sookie: So, how do I look?

Bill: You look like vampire bait.

Sookie: So, you're saying I look nice?

While the rest of Europe was wrestling with revolution, Germany was firmly sunk in aristocratic torpor. Until the end of the nineteenth century, there was no real country called "Germany." Instead, there was a patchwork collection of duchies and principalities, of which the most important was Prussia. German philosophic thinkers of the late eighteenth and nineteenth centuries were often less interested in political questions than they were in abstract thought. This makes their writing very difficult to read today, something we'll come up against again when we talk about Georg Wilhelm Friedrich Hegel in the next chapter. But Immanuel Kant is quite hard enough to start with.

Immanuel Kant (1724–1804) was born in Prussia in what is now the town of Kaliningrad in Russia. He was a typically anal-retentive German, taking a walk at three-thirty every afternoon on the dot, so punctual that local housewives would set their clocks by him. He never married, never left Prussia, and rarely stepped outside his own home town. And it was not until he entered his late fifties that he developed his enduring philosophical ideas. So, there's hope for some of us yet....

Kant considered a lot of philosophical problems, including the existence or nonexistence of God and the question of what sorts of things we know innately as opposed to what we know as a result of experience. But let's start by talking about Kant's theory of morality.

MORAL AUTONOMY

Kant had a raging intellectual bent for what he called "moral auton-omy." Only we humans have this capacity. We have transcended the rest of the animal kingdom because we are able to make free, auton-omous decisions, while our furry little nonhuman friends are slaves to instinct, incapable of making decisions based on the imperatives of morality. Animals only make "decisions" based on the dictates of nature's instruction. Kant sums up his human-centric philosophy:

> **"Morality, and humanity insofar as it is capable of morality, is that which alone has dignity."**

Ouch. Take that, Fluffy. Kant considers these nonhuman animals to be things, to be used as we see fit for our benefit. Every animal from a dolphin to the family dog has absolutely no dignity. Thus, these animals have no inherent value whatsoever, but only have a value insofar as they are useful to us, a value determined by how useful they are. They have a price. Hmm, no wonder Michael Vick quoted Kant during his defense in court.

Ed, the talking horse who starred in *Mr. Ed*, would disagree, of course. But then Ed saw himself as something other than a run-of-the-mill animal.

[Wilbur finds Mister Ed sleeping in his living room]

Wilbur: Oh no.

Mister Ed: If you had a dog, you'd let him sleep in the house.

Wilbur: A dog is different. A dog is a household pet.

Mister Ed: Then call me "Rover" and wake me at eight.

A HORSE IS A HORSE, OF COURSE, OF COURSE . . .
Inquisitive viewers of *Mr. Ed*, which ran from 1961 to 1966, might have wondered from time to time how Ed's mouth moved when he "talked." Some associated with the show claimed that the horse was trained to bare its teeth when someone tapped his or her foot. The more believable explanation given is that clear elastic cords were attached to a bridle bit that ran under Ed's lip. When the cameramen wanted him to talk, someone pulled on the cords. That's television magic.

Human beings, on the other hand, according to Kant, cannot use other human beings without their consent. One of the most important formulations of Kant's supreme moral principle, "the categorical imperative," is the "Formula of the End in Itself." Kant believes humans should treat other humans as an end in themselves, not as some useful stepping stone to some other goal.

> "Act as if the maxim of your action were to become through your will a general natural law."
> —Immanuel Kant

We cannot use others as a means to attain some other object. Because all humans, as rational autonomous people, share the ability to follow their own goals and pursue their own dreams, we must get consent if we want something from someone or want to do something to someone—like turn them into a friggin' vampire.

To Be . . . Undead or Not to Be . . . Undead

Many of us wish we could be vampires. They're immortal, thin (that's what comes of a mostly liquid diet), and they have a certain dangerous sex appeal. Plus, they are the only ones that seem to look better without a tan. Many of us mere mortals, it seems, suffer from fang envy, which is why stories of these bloodthirsty bandits continue to fascinate us.

THE WEIRDEST TV VAMPIRES EVER

For all their popularity in literature and the movies, vampires haven't turned up on television as often as you might think. One of the more notable instances was in the twisted soap opera *Dark Shadows*. The show aired on

ABC from 1966 to 1971 and starred Joan Bennett and the briefly famous Jonathan Frid. The latter played Barnabas Collins, a 200-year-old vampire. Unfortunately, the show's microscopic production budget meant that each episode had to be videotaped in live performance, with no re-takes, and that production values were nonexistent. The results were hilarious—actors regularly flubbed their lines and bumped into the scenery. Matters reached a crescendo when in a flashback showing Barnabas infected by a vampire bat, a rubber bat on a clearly visible string was swung down from above camera range, while Jonathan Frid grabbed it, jammed it against his throat, and let out a blood-curdling series of growling shrieks.

But it is one thing to dress like Count Dracula on Halloween or at a gothic club on the weekends, and it is quite another thing to be a vampire permanently. It is a major life decision, like going to college or getting a calf implant. *True Blood*'s Bill knows this well, which is why he can't seem to bring himself to turn his beloved Sookie into a monster like him—unless she agrees.

JUST WHO IS BILL?

Bill (a great name for a vampire by the way) was born in 1835, and his children were born before the Civil War. On November 20, 1868, he was made a vampire by Lorena, with whom he had a tempestuous affair. "Vampire Bill" is also the creator of a valuable and highly controversial database listing all the vampires in North America.

Bill wrestles with this Kantian dilemma. Should he turn his love into a fellow vampire? What if he is certain that she will like it—does that make a difference? After all, Social Security for thousands of years doesn't sound that bad. Kant, arms sternly folded, says no. The action is only permissible with the consent of both rational entities, two persons in the Kantian sense. (If it were a matter of turning Mr. Ed into a vampire, Bill would find Kant a lot more flexible—although even in that case there might be questions.) Bill must accord Sookie and all his fellow rational agents the respect they deserve. Now, if she chooses to make his goal as her own, that is, if she *chooses* to become the vampiric vixen that he so desires, well, according to Kant, that's her own doing.

But What about Jessica?

The philosophical plot thickens when you consider the character of Jessica, a woman who, despite fighting like the dickens to avoid being turned into a creature of the night, is arguably better off as a vampire than she was in her normal, mortal existence. Her vampire family has certainly empowered her in a way her moral family never could have. So, do we ever have a right to do something against another's wishes because we know it will be in their best interests?

> "I want to kill people. I'm so hungry, and all you do is talk, and I'm starving. You're so mean! You're supposed to take care of me. That's what you said. And, oh, you SUCK! Hahahahahahaha. That's funny because you do suck."
> —Jessica to Bill, *True Blood*

Take the paternalistic laws that exist in our own society, like the motorcycle helmet law. Unlike driving drunk, wearing a motorcycle helmet won't have any effect on the lives of others. So why do we have this law? Because the freedom of not wearing a motorcycle helmet is an unimportant one, we figure, and if forcing people to wear helmets—a minor inconvenience—saves even one life, it is worth it.

But Kant has a point: We have to be careful in making such decisions. Think of one of the arguments the government relied on for going into Iraq: We were doing it "for the Iraqi people's freedom." If the majority of Iraqis don't want us there, that is beside the point. Eventually, they'll see it was in their best interests. Of course, democracy isn't much use to a person who's dead.

Though we can imagine specific situations in which we might conclude it best to force someone into doing something for his or her own good, Kant believes we must not take such action. He's absolute in his assertion that we must respect other autonomous wills.

Who Can Use Whom?

There is another philosophical issue raised in *True Blood,* one that Kant might be able to help us with. Kant—like many philosophers before him—philosophically justifies our human right to dominion over the animals. Some philosophers, like René Descartes, even argued that animals could not feel pain, and therefore killing them doesn't even count as taking a life. But what if there were vampires who viewed humans the way we view animals?

Vampires in *True Blood* are superior to humans in every way. Physically, they blow us out of the water. They are stronger, their senses are more cultivated, and they live forever. Intellectually, they make us look like complete idiots. It is no wonder, then, that in *True Blood,* humans seek to emulate the experience of being a vampire—just not with the whole bite-the-neck-and-die-but-live-for-eternity thing. They do this by sampling vampire blood.

One sip of vampire blood, or V juice, and you can get a small taste of what being a bad-ass vampire is like. Sookie realizes this when she takes a sip of Bill's blood. Her senses are suddenly on superhuman overdrive, the simple act of eating a basic sausage breakfast is nothing short of divine. "It's like I can see the farm the pig lived on, and feel the sun and rain on my face, and even taste the earth that the herbs grew out of . . . ." Top that, IHoP.

Vampires, it seems, have us beat both mentally and physically. And they know it, which is why they consider humans a lowly life form, akin to animals. This is why Bill gets in big trouble in the vampire community when he stakes his fellow vampire, Longshadow, to save his human hottie, Sookie. "You killed a higher life form to save your pet," the magister says, obviously appalled and confused by such an act. Humans are to be used purely as a means to satisfy vampires. As Lorena says to Bill, "You are vampire. They are food." Pam, a less than charming vampire, goes so far as calling humans "pathetic lumps of temporary flesh." Damn, that's harsh.

But vampires are not the only ones guilty of speciesism. Humans in *True Blood* consider themselves to be superior to vampires, though they'll do anything to get their hands on some V juice. On what basis do they believe themselves superior? Morality. Humans, good Kantians, believe that they are good, and the vampires are evil.

Do Vamps Have Rights?

The Fellowship of the Sun, a Dallas-based church that provides an important plot arc in the show, affords no rights to vampires because they are evil. Why are they evil? Sure, they may be able to leap buildings in a single bound and speed-read *War and Peace*, but they are not capable of moral reasoning. If they were, how could they do something as morally repugnant as devouring human flesh?

The vampire's response is that human flesh is to them what cow flesh is to us. We might feel different about beef if we stopped to consider it from the cow's point of view. If we expect vampires, a superior species, to treat us with dignity, as an end rather than a means, why don't humans afford animals similar respect? From this standpoint, a vampire has just as much right to eat a human as we have to eat a cow.

Philosophy for Thought

Kant, in his various writings, never defines precisely what constitutes personhood (remember that debate in *Star Trek: The Next Generation* about Data?). In thinking about Kant's moral system, are we justified in asking whether or not a person in a coma has any dignity? What about a person suffering from a significant mental deficiency? Are they by definition totally devoid of any dignity, devoid of any inherent value? Do they cease to be persons, with the ability to make moral judgments?

The same scenario can be used to challenge most of the definitions of personhood by history's most notable philosophers. Even for Plato, man is a "rational animal," and his access to Reason stands between him and the animal world. But how this would apply to a person in a coma or suffering from a mental disability is not clear.

GOD AND HERR KANT

Kant is sometimes called the Father of Agnosticism. He refused to accept that there is a purely rational basis for believing in God. His answer comes in his book *Critique of Practical Reason*, in which he argues that belief in God guarantees a system of morality that will lead to happiness. Therefore, even if God doesn't exist, we should believe in him. It's this sort of doubletalk that makes Kant an irritating philosopher to read, even when he's got something interesting to say.

Kant is deeply critical of the practices of Christianity that he observed in his native Prussia. But concerning the *actual* existence of God, he holds that it's not possible to prove it one way or the other. We can only think of the existence of God as something that's necessitated by our need for happiness. Another eighteenth-century thinker, Voltaire, said, "If God did not exist, it would be necessary to invent him."

This issue is the subject of an episode of *Barney Miller*. The show, which ran from 1975 to 1982, was set in Precinct 12 of the New York Police Force, located in Greenwich Village. The squad of detectives was headed by Captain Barney Miller (Hal Linden), and included Harris (Ron Glass), Wojciehowicz (Max Gail), and Dietrich (Steve Landesberg). The latter was the intellectual of the squad room and could always be counted on to supply whatever out-of-the-way information was needed.

At one point Dietrich asks Barney, "Captain, do you believe in God?"

Barney: Well, I always thought there was something . . . .

Dietrich: I don't. I think we're just a bunch of absurd people put here for no reason.

Barney: Yeah? And what if you're wrong? What if you get up there, and there's God. What do you say to him?

Dietrich: [after thinking] "Oops!"

CHAPTER 12
Reading Hegel in Outer Space

Of all the philosophers of the nineteenth century, nobody's harder to understand than the Germans. And of the Germans, nobody wrote denser, more indecipherable prose than Georg Wilhelm Friedrich Hegel. This is too bad, because he's also been very influential. Karl Marx read Hegel's stuff while studying at university and turned it into one of the most powerful political movements of the twentieth century. Americans including Ralph Waldo Emerson and the Transcendentalists were influenced by Hegel's ideas.

In this chapter we'll look at the broad outline of Hegel's philosophy, and we'll consider it through the lens of *Star Trek: Deep Space Nine*.

BEING A PHILOSOPHER CAN BE REALLY, REALLY BORING

Hegel (1770–1831) is a good example of the fact that interesting philosophers often lead lives of mind-numbing boredom. He taught philosophy at a private school, then at the University of Heidelberg, and finally at the University of Berlin. When he was young, he admired Napoleon, who was then conquering much of Europe. But by the time he got to be older, he became a very patriotic Prussian and hated Napoleon and his legacy.

Napoleon is a good thing to keep in the back of your mind while reading about Hegel, because it's useful to remember that while Hegel was writing his books, especially his early and most important book, *The Phenomenology of Mind*, massive changes were taking place around him. Napoleon had consolidated the revolution-wracked France into a powerful state, built an army, and started on the creation of an empire that would, at its height, stretch from Vienna to Madrid.

With all of this in mind, it's not surprising that some of the philosophic questions that Hegel was most preoccupied with were those regarding change and freedom.

The Power of the Dialectic

One of the most important concepts that Hegel developed was the idea of "the Whole." He believed that we have to conceive of the universe and its component parts as a single entity. This wholeness—and this is where things get tricky—is purely the creation of Reason. To the degree that we use our reason, we become a greater part of reality.

> **"The real is rational, and the rational is real."**
> —G. W. F. Hegel

If we're going to think of something as whole, though, we have to be able to see it not as it is at any given stage of its existence, but as a process. Hegel believes that everything is a progression toward what he calls the Absolute, which exists in the mind of God. Through this progression, the notion of change embeds itself in Hegel's philosophy and never lets go. The structure of this progression is what he calls the "dialectic," which is a three-part process:

- **Step One.** *Thesis.* This is a statement about something.
- **Step Two.** *Antithesis.* This is a statement about the something that is necessitated by the thesis but that contradicts it.
- **Step Three.** *Synthesis.* This is a reconciliation of the thesis and antithesis, which subsumes both of them into itself and produces something new, something that is a further development from them.

Let's look at two examples—one from Hegel's philosophy and the other from television. First, Hegel's philosophy:

- *Thesis.* The Absolute is pure Being. Well, that's clear enough. For the Absolute to be Absolute, it can't really have any definable qualities, because that would limit it. But on the other hand, if it doesn't have any qualities, to all intents and purposes it doesn't exist. So we're led to . . .
- *Antithesis.* The Absolute is Nothing. But this contradicts the thesis. How can the Absolute be Being and Nothing at the same time? We need the . . .
- *Synthesis.* The Absolute is Becoming. Okay, now we've got it. Being and Nothing fuse to form Becoming. The Absolute is always in a state of Becoming.

Okay, maybe that wasn't so clear. Let's look at another example.

Odo the Shape Changer

Star Trek: Deep Space Nine was the third Star Trek series (there was the original series back in the sixties and then *Star Trek: The Next Generation*, which ran from 1987 to 1994). *Deep Space Nine*, starring Avery Brooks, ran from 1993 to 1999, and was darker, grimmer, and in general better written than the previous *Star Trek* series. It was set aboard a space station located in a politically explosive area of the galaxy—a kind of frontier town where rival factions watched one another with narrowed eyes, phasers always at the ready.

Keeping the peace is Constable Odo (René Auberjonois), who has to constantly watch races such as the Bajorans, the Cardassians, and the Ferengi (especially the Ferengi) as they struggle for control of the station and the wormhole in space located near it.

Odo is a shape changer, a kind of creature that no one in the *Star Trek* universe knows much about. He was found abandoned on a planet and raised in a laboratory by the Cardassians. He can assume any shape, animate or inanimate, an ability that makes him a formidable foe of wrongdoers aboard *Deep Space Nine*.

THE WONDERS OF MORPHING

The fact that *Deep Space Nine* could feature a character such as Odo was due to evolving television technology: in specific, the technique of morphing, changing one image seamlessly into another. TV and movie special-effects wizards began using it in the early 1990s, notably in the movie *Terminator 2: Judgment Day*. *Deep Space Nine* was the first television show to make extensive use of the technique.

Odo versus Quark

Let's take a typical scenario from the show—one that pits Odo against his chief criminal opponent, Quark, the Ferengi who runs a bar/gambling parlor/brothel aboard the station.

Quark is sitting calmly in his rooms, chatting with a group of three visitors. The subject of their talk: Quark's cut of a consignment of smuggled spices and narcotics. Quark wants to make sure he's paid exactly what it's worth in pressed latinum. Quark's none-too-bright brother, Rom, enters with a tray of drinks and starts to hand them out. Suddenly, and without warning, one of the glasses on the tray trembles, shifting its shape, spreading out along the tray and knocking the hapless Rom feet over giant ears. The shape spreads into a tall, slender form and becomes Odo. He grips Quark by the ear lobe.

"Now I've got you!" he hisses.

Quark glares at Rom.

"Four people in the room," he squeals in fury, "*and you didn't notice there were five glasses on the tray!*"

All right. In Hegelian terms, what just happened?

The Thesis was the fifth glass. It had all the external appearance of a glass; in fact, it looked exactly like the others on the tray. But within its molecular structure, it was quite different. As Rom handed round drinks, Odo began to shift his shape. He "negated"—to use another Hegelian term—the glass and assumed instead his own shape, his true shape. This was the Antithesis.

But wait! Since Odo can become anything he wants, his shape as Odo (or, if you like, René Auberjonois) isn't in fact his true shape. We have to understand Odo as a process of *becoming* other shapes. This insight allows us to have a truer and more complete understanding of who or what Odo is. He isn't any one thing; he's anything he chooses to become.

Odo is the Hegelian dialectic personified.

TRANSFORMATION IS THE ESSENCE OF EXISTENCE

Hegel breaks away from the idea that phenomena must be considered as static reality. Remember when we talked about the Law of Identity back in Chapter 5? We said that by the terms of the law, a thing had to be itself or something else—it couldn't be both. Lucille Ball and Harpo Marx had to be Lucille Ball and Harpo Marx when they were performing the mirror routine on *I Love Lucy*—one couldn't be the other, even if they looked like each other and mistook each other for reflections.

Hegel stands the Law of Identity on its head. He says, yes, something *can* be both itself and something else. Lucy *can* be herself and Harpo. She can be perceived by us as *becoming* Harpo, just as Harpo can be seen becoming Lucy.

This viewpoint makes everything that we thought was firm and solid under our feet suddenly feel as if it's shifting and uncertain. No wonder Hegel's writings inspired generations of philosophers to argue with one another. And no wonder, as we'll see in a subsequent chapter, that one of his most ardent disciples was a young German student named Karl Marx.

CHAPTER 13

John Stuart Mill and the Utilitarian Heroism of Dexter Morgan

"Actions are right in proportion as they tend to promote happiness; wrong as they tend to produce the reverse of happiness."
—John Stuart Mill

"Am I evil? Am I good? I'm done asking those questions. I don't have the answers. Does anyone?"
—Dexter Morgan

Beginning in the late eighteenth century, the technological movement that we call the Industrial Revolution began. Workers migrated from the countryside to the cities, where they crowded into dirty factories, which belched smoke and soot into the air as engines pounded and looms clacked.

Philosophers (along with everyone else in Europe and America) tried to come to grips with this vast change, which remade the landscape and changed human relations forever. In the next couple of chapters, we'll see some of the ways in which thinkers tried to understand what was going on and what it meant for the old ways of thinking. In this chapter, we'll look at one of the most important attempts to do this, the English philosophic movement called Utilitarianism. Even though the movement largely died out by the beginning of the twentieth century, it was extremely popular in mid-nineteenth-century Britain, Germany, and France.

To understand how Utilitarianism works, we'll enlist the aid of a fascinating companion: Dexter Morgan.

A SERIAL KILLER FOR MOTHER

Dexter Morgan is America's favorite murderer. He's good looking, well dressed, well mannered, smart, funny. He'd be the perfect guy to take home to mom if he weren't a cold-blooded killer.

Dexter is a sociopath. This is clear from the beginning of the series of the same name, which has been running since 2006 on Showtime. Dexter's inner monologues give us direct access into the mind of a murderer, a man who learned early on that he was different from his fellow humans, unable to connect with them in any meaningful way. When he is forced to interact, he fakes it, to keep up the appearance of normalcy, critical to his survival. But it isn't easy.

> **"I can kill a man, dismember his body, and be home in time for Letterman. But knowing what to say when my girlfriend's feeling insecure ... I'm totally lost."**
> —Dexter

When we meet Dexter, he has no natural interest in basic human desires, like the desire for sex or love or friendship. However, as Dexter evolves, he begins to question the conventional wisdom of his inability to connect to others.

> **"I just know there's something dark in me and I hide it. I certainly don't talk about it, but it's there always, this Dark Passenger. And when he's driving, I feel alive, half sick with the thrill of complete wrongness. I don't fight him, I don't want to. He's all I've got. Nothing else could love me, not even ... especially not me. Or is that just a lie the Dark Passenger tells me? Because lately there are these moments when I feel connected to something else ... someone. It's like the mask is slipping and things ... people ... who never mattered before are suddenly starting to matter. It scares the hell out of me."**
>
> —Dexter

Despite his personal evolution, one thing always remains the same: Dexter needs to kill. His blood lust must be satisfied.

Does It Matter Why Dex Does It?

While the motivation for his menacing murders is his innate desire to kill, Dexter has found a way to channel his killer instinct in a socially useful direction: He wants to rid the world of bad guys who have successfully evaded the law. Dexter's desire to kill might not be innocent, but neither are the people he kills. So the show's premise centers on one question: Is Dexter Morgan a vigilante hero making the world a better and more just place or is he really just a bloodthirsty, cold-blooded killer?

The answer depends on whom you ask, but if the Utilitarian philosophers John Stuart Mill (1806–1873) and Jeremy Bentham (1748–1842) could tune in, they'd most certainly root for Dexter.

Bentham was a London-born child prodigy who started studying Latin at the ripe old age of three. A bona fide liberal, he advocated equal rights for women, the separation of church and state, free speech, the right to divorce, and was even a strong proponent of animal rights and the decriminalization of homosexuality.

BENTHAM VERSUS JEFFERSON IN A CAGE MATCH

Interestingly, for all his liberal political positions, Bentham was opposed to the American Revolution. In particular, Bentham was a critic of the concept of "inalienable rights," as spelled out in Jefferson's Declaration of Independence. Bentham argued that rights derive from the actions of the government itself and can be taken away by the government. Bentham famously referred to the doctrine of Natural Rights as "nonsense on stilts."

The crux of Utilitarianism, according to Bentham, is the idea that moral actions are those that prove useful in producing the "greatest good for the greatest number of people." By "good" Bentham meant "pleasure/happiness" or "happiness," and by "bad" he meant the "absence of pleasure/happiness." While this is sometimes called "ethical hedonism," Bentham is not viewing pleasure in the purely sensorial way that a real hedonist would. In other words, Bentham would probably object to a group of weirdos killing an innocent person simply because they find murder to be orgasmic.

> **"It is the greatest good to the greatest number of people which is the measure of right and wrong."**
> —Jeremy Bentham

Bentham's Moral Calculator

Bentham formulated a moral algorithm called the "calculus of felicity" to calculate the degree or amount of pleasure that an action is likely to cause. Included in this calculation were different variables, which Bentham called "dimensions" or "elements." Among these were:

- *Intensity*: How strong is the pleasure?
- *Duration*: How long will the pleasure last?
- *Certainty or uncertainty*: How likely or unlikely is it that the pleasure will occur?
- *Propinquity or remoteness*: How soon will the pleasure occur?
- *Fecundity*: The probability that the action will be followed by sensations of the same kind.
- *Purity*: The probability that it will not be followed by sensations of the opposite kind.
- *Extent*: How many people will be affected?

Taking our example of a group of lunatics who find murdering innocent people produces ecstasy, we can see that this does not pass the "purity" test. While the killers might get off on murder, the person being murdered is experiencing what can only be considered a less than orgasmic feeling (i.e., dying)—unless you're David Carradine.

John Stuart Mill, Bentham's pupil and protégé, took Utilitarianism to the next level. His major contribution to Utilitarian philosophical thought is his qualitative analysis of different pleasures. Not all good feeling should be treated equally. A night at the opera produces a feeling of pleasure superior to that of a game of hopscotch, argued Mill, apparently having no knack for fancy footwork. Unlike Bentham, Mill believed that the character and quality of each pleasure produced needs to be judged to determine the morality of an act. Mill's famous quote, "better to be Socrates dissatisfied than a fool satisfied," sums up this hierarchical view of pleasure.

Mill started off with an background befitting a nineteenth-century, London-born society figure. His father, James Mill, gave him an excellent education, so that John learned Greek at the age of three, Latin at eight. James Mill, a well-known liberal reformer, belonged to the same group, called the "philosophical radicals," as Jeremy Bentham. For years he was Bentham's chief assistant and philosophic defender. So it was only natural that John Stuart Mill would be sympathetic to Utilitarianism.

"We can never be sure that the opinion we are endeavouring to stifle is a false opinion; and if we were sure, stifling it would be an evil still."
—John Stuart Mill

NOT ALL PLEASURES ARE EQUAL

As Utilitarianism developed at the hands of Bentham, James Mill, and John Stuart Mill, it was divided between Act Utilitarianism and Rule Utilitarianism.

1. The Act Utilitarian believes that each moral dilemma should be considered separately in order to determine whether it stands up to the Utilitarian morality test.
2. A Rule Utilitarian believes that the Utilitarian metric for determining the rightness or wrongness of an action should be used to develop basic rules or laws for us to live by.

Dexter Kills Serial Killers

An Act Utilitarian could make a very solid case that Dexter is saving lives by murdering psychopaths and that his actions are therefore in the interest of the public. This meets the test of maximizing pleasure and minimizing pain for the greatest number of people. However, a Rule Utilitarian might have a harder time defending Dexter's extracurricular exploits. How do you legitimize vigilantism—which is what Dexter is doing—without destroying the social compact under which we've all agreed to live? Surely society is better off without the people he kills. But isn't he doing it in the wrong way and for the wrong reasons? Isn't there something disturbing about a guy gratifying his blood lust, even in the interests of a more just society?

Many of us feel this ambivalence watching Dexter. We might think that his murderous behavior is just, but few of us would suggest that the police should let him go if he is caught. We recognize the value of having a rule that states "Murder is wrong" even if it means that our pal Dexter would be punished for his actions. We are willing to accept that there will be an increase in aggregate utility or "good" if the rule that prohibits murder in all forms is adhered to universally. According to this logic, if there is no law that prevents vigilantes like Dexter from taking the law into their own hands, the general "good" will diminish, even if some bad people are taken off the streets. More innocent people might die if Dexter is jailed, but in the long run a Rule Utilitarian would argue that more people would die if there were more Dexters.

Notice, by the way, the difference between the Utilitarian approach to this issue and that of our old friend Immanuel Kant, who, because of the existence of an unalterable moral imperative that's implanted in us (whether by God or something else; but Kant believes we should say it's God, even if it isn't), would condemn Dexter out of hand. There's a moral imperative against murder under all circumstances. This exists quite apart from its effects on society, something Kant's not really interested in.

Can We Bring Them Together?

There is, however, an argument that Act and Rule Utilitarianism are not incompatible. Think of our murder laws as they exist right now. Murder is illegal except in the event of self-defense. A Rule Utilitarian may not be able to make exceptions to the rule as in the Dexter case, but, not being a Kantian, he can still make rules that enable self-defense and are exceptions to a general prohibition of murder. This isn't really breaking the rules—pun intended—it just means we have to be careful in how we phrase our general prohibition against murder.

For instance, instead of writing a law that says, "Killing another person is wrong," we could say, "Killing another person is wrong except in the act of self-defense." And to help our friend Dexter, why not write a law that says, "Killing another person is wrong except if you're murdering murderers"? Both the Act and Rule Utilitarian, then, could embrace Dexter's unique form of justice.

DECODING DEXTER'S CODE

Recognizing his uncontrollable blood lust, Dexter's adoptive father, Harry, a police officer, dedicated himself to training his sociopathic son to channel his love of the kill for good rather than evil.

Harry: Okay, so we can't stop this. But maybe . . . we can do something . . . to channel it. Use it for good.

Teenage Dexter: How could it ever be good?

Harry: Son, there are people out there who do really bad things. Terrible people. And the police can't catch them all. Do you understand what I'm saying?

Teenage Dexter: You're saying . . . they deserve it.

The show is centered on Dexter's struggle to adhere to this maxim. As Harry says, "Killing must serve a purpose. Otherwise, it's just plain murder." By nature, Dexter is a monster (or at least he thinks he is). By nurture, he is a dark knight, a violator of violators, the enforcer of the Code of Harry.

So, can the Code of Harry be defended on Utilitarian moral grounds?

Well, the first rule of the code, "Don't get caught," is less about exerting justice and more directly about saving Dexter's ass, which is hardly a moral maxim. However, we can consider that Dexter is an instrument of justice, and we don't want the instrument broken, since if it is, it can't function anymore. Therefore, we'll pass the first rule—but we'll come back to this in a minute, because it raises a significant problem for Bentham and Utilitarian thought.

The second rule of the code is to "be sure" of the guilt of Dexter's victims so that an innocent man isn't killed. This is easily defendable from any moral philosophical viewpoint.

The Trolley Problem

The first rule of the code is a little more tricky, but still defendable. The Utilitarian might argue that if Dexter gets caught by the police, the result will be an aggregate loss of pleasure in the world as he will no longer be able to rid society of these vicious killers. But—and here's the problem—does this mean the Utilitarian has to condone everything Dexter does to avoid capture? If Dexter has to kill an innocent person in order to remain free, should a Utilitarian oppose this on moral grounds even if it means more innocent people will die in the long term if Dexter is caught? Can you kill one innocent person to save 100? Intuitively, most of us as good Utilitarians would agree in the abstract that you can and that in fact you should.

The philosopher Philippa Foot (1920–2010) put the problem very succinctly in a form that's come to be called the Trolley Problem.

"A trolley is running out of control down a track. In its path are five people who have been tied to the track by a mad philosopher. Fortunately, you could flip a switch, which will lead the trolley down a different track to safety. Unfortunately, there is a single person tied to that track. Should you flip the switch or do nothing?"

Utilitarians would argue that sending the trolley careening toward the single person would save five lives at the cost of one and therefore contribute to the greatest happiness of the greatest number. Our instinct is to agree with that, but something feels wrong about it. What happens if we change the stakes? Consider the following scenario: There are two buttons you can press. One will kill one person, one will kill a million. You have to press one. What do you do?

Easy, right? But suppose you make it two million people with one button and three million people with the other? What then? Do you want to commit mass murder? Does the number of people involved even matter? From a Utilitarian standpoint it does. From a Kantian outlook, it doesn't.

Utilitarianism in Baghdad

This sort of problem isn't abstract; it has applications in real life. Consider one of the arguments used to make the case for war in Iraq. After weapons of mass destruction—the original cause for going to war—failed to show up, some sophisticated political thinkers justified the war on the grounds that ridding the nation of Saddam Hussein would lead to a freer and more prosperous democratic Iraq. Former president George W. Bush and like-minded cohorts are convinced that one day, when Iraq is a model democracy, their efforts will be vindicated. So far, this has come at the cost of more than 100,000 Iraqi lives as well as those of at least 4,400 American soldiers. Even if a democratic Iraq is eventually created out of all this chaos, does it justify waging a war and causing havoc and horror in the short term? Democracy is a great thing, but it doesn't matter much to you when you're dead.

"The only purpose for which power can be rightfully exercised over any member of a civilized community, against his will, is to prevent harm to others."

John Stuart Mill saw this problem in Utilitarianism. Bentham, he felt, had developed a principle that means individuals have a right to do as they please unless their actions harm others. Mill, however, says, Hmm, anyone seen Dexter?

Mill's increased focus on individual liberty tried to offer a way to get around the moral dilemma stated in the Trolley Problem. His failure to find an adequate solution is one reason Utilitarianism isn't with us today.

DEXTER MORGAN'S MORAL DUTY

Does it matter what motivates Dexter to kill? Does it matter what we feel inside, or is what we do the only thing that's important?

> "Harry and Doris did a wonderful job raising me. But they're both dead now. I didn't kill them. Honest."
> —Dexter

To a moral philosopher like Kant, motivation certainly does matter. Kant believed that the only purely good thing was the good will. Intention matters more than consequences of the actions themselves. And most of us can't help but feel that it *does* matter why Dexter is killing.

I would argue that Dexter is motivated toward the good. Harry taught him right and wrong, and he struggles to follow the code. Dexter feels a deep sense of duty to obey this code, which is revealed in his discussions with the spirit of his late adoptive father. This sense of duty to follow a moral code is similar to the Kantian idea of a moral duty to the categorical imperative, the supreme moral law. While the Code of Harry is nothing like Kant's categorical imperative or the moral laws of the Ten Commandments in content, the idea that there are objective moral laws in the universe that must be followed rests on the same philosophical foundation.

CHAPTER 14

Karl Marx and Adam Smith, Meet Alex P. Keaton

"The real tragedy of the poor is the poverty
of their aspirations."
—Adam Smith, *The Wealth of Nations*

"Philosophers have only interpreted the world in various
ways. The point, however, is to change it."
—Karl Marx, "Theses on Feuerbach"

"If you put your mind to it, you can accomplish anything."
—Alex P. Keaton, *Family Ties*

By the middle of the nineteenth century, industrialism had taken firm root not only in Europe but in the United States. In 1869, the last spike of the Intercontinental Railroad was driven in, linking the eastern and western coasts of North America. From Berlin to San Francisco, factories and mills churned out goods that were carried around the world.

This vast expansion of human productivity brought with it immense wealth—for a select few. Philosophers, hitherto relatively disinterested observers of society, now became intimately involved in movements for social change. No one embodied this more than Karl Marx (1818–1883) and his long-time collaborator Friedrich Engels (1820–1895).

ROSEANNE BECOMES A MARXIST (WELL, NOT REALLY)

Marx and Engels were disciples of Hegel, but they took his thinking in a radically new direction. Hegel had seen the dialectical process as working in the abstract, moving toward a culmination in the Absolute Spirit. Marx believed that he could apply this method to the actual working out of history. Influenced by the liberal movements of the mid-nineteenth century, he and Engels developed an idea of historical progress in which each social system, containing within it the seeds of its own destruction, was eventually overthrown and replaced. As Hegel saw the world progressing toward Absolute Spirit, Marx viewed it as progressing toward communism.

> "The history of all hitherto existing society is the history of class struggles."
> —Karl Marx and Friedrich Engels, *The Communist Manifesto*

Marx became convinced that what drove social progress was the conflict between classes—classes defined by their relationship to the means of production. Workers, the overwhelming majority of society, sold their labor power in return for wages. Capitalists bought this labor power and used it to create profit, which they appropriated to themselves.

To understand this, consider the sitcom *Roseanne*, starring Roseanne Barr. The show ran from 1988 to 1997 and made a star not only out of Roseanne but out of John Goodman, who played her husband. It was unusual in its day since neither Barr nor Goodman were physically attractive (at least by the television standards of the day), and the show dealt with the ups and downs of an ordinary working-class family.

WHY DOES TV HATE WORKING PEOPLE?

TV has always been reluctant to show people who are working class. Most television protagonists tend to have unspecified jobs that aren't important to the plot (think of Chandler on *Friends* or Barney Stinson on *How I Met Your Mother*); work for themselves (Tim Taylor on *Home Improvement*, or Alan Harper and Charlie Harper on *Two and a Half Men*); or are independent "artists" (Jerry Seinfeld on *Seinfeld*). A real working-class hero is unusual.

In season one, Roseanne and her sister Jackie (Laurie Metcalf) are employed as line workers at Wellman Plastics. In Marxist terms, they are selling to Wellman their ability to create value (in the form of plastic objects). Wellman purchases this ability and, in return, pays them a wage.

But Roseanne and Jackie and the other employees of Wellman Plastics create more value in a given period than they receive in wages. This "surplus value," as Marx calls it, is appropriated by the owners of Wellman. Some of it they spend on raw materials, some they spend on plant upkeep, taxes, and so on. But some portion of it is profit, which they keep for themselves.

None of this has anything to do with whether the owners of Wellman are bad people or Roseanne and Jackie are good. In fact, Jackie has a brief relationship with the foreman at the factory (played by George Clooney, of all people!). Marx argues that it's the nature of the capitalist system to exploit workers—by which he means, capitalism pays workers less than the full value of what they produce and takes the surplus value for itself.

Marx wants to see a system in which Jackie, Roseanne, and their fellow workers will, through the state, own the plastics factory. Some portion of the value they produce will still have to go to raw materials and other things, but—and this is the important point—the part of value that was previously owned privately as profit will now be owned socially. In Hegelian terms, the thesis of capitalism confronts the antithesis of the working class. After a struggle between these two forces, they are replaced by a synthesis: socialism, eventually leading to communism.

THE GHOST OF ADAM SMITH

Marx spent most of his life living in exile from his native Germany. He settled in London, where he was largely supported financially by Engels, who had inherited a string of factories in England (and don't think you're the first one to find the irony in the fathers of communism being financially kept afloat by the profits of capitalist factories). There he buried himself in the British Library Reading Room, where he researched his magnum opus, *Capital*.

Capital is primarily a work of economics, though it has some interesting philosophical sidelights. Marx left Engels to write about philosophy—and pretty much everything else—while he concentrated on economic theory. In this, he absorbed information and lessons from some of the great British economists of the eighteenth and nineteenth century. The most important of these was a Scot, Adam Smith.

Considered today the father of capitalism, Smith was a revolutionary thinker. While today we think his free-market principles are representative of "conservative" economic policies, in his own time Adam Smith's laissez-faire economic theory forever changed the West's perception of economic trade.

Born in Kirkcaldy, Fife, Scotland, around 1723, Smith was appointed professor of logic at Glasgow University in 1751. In 1776, he wrote what would become his most famous work, *The Wealth of Nations*. In 1759 he published *The Theory of Moral Sentiments*. And in 1778, he was appointed to a post of commissioner of customs in Edinburgh, Scotland. He died there on July 17, 1790. Upon his death it was discovered that the die-hard capitalist had devoted a considerable part of his income to numerous secret acts of charity.

ENLIGHTENMENT AND HAGGIS

Smith was part of what is called the Scottish Enlightenment. In the eighteenth century, what is called simply "the Enlightenment"—a great outburst of liberal learning and philosophical theorizing—mainly developed in France, among people like Voltaire, Diderot, Rousseau, Montesquieu, and others like them. But there was a significant parallel movement in Scotland, which produced Smith, David Hume, the poet Robert Burns, the novelist Walter Scott, and others.

People such as Benjamin Franklin and Thomas Jefferson were familiar with the works of writers in both France and Scotland, and it influenced them a great deal. So the American Revolution and the French Revolution can both be considered the political outcome of the Enlightenment.

During Smith's time, the European powers, like Smith's native Britain, accepted and practiced the economic theory of mercantilism. The core of this idea was that the larger a nation's trade surplus relative to other nations, the more economically powerful and wealthier that nation would be. In other words, if you could make everyone in every other country buy your products and not buy any of theirs, you win and they lose.

If that were the case today, we'd have to say that China is kicking the ass of everyone on the planet. The fact that we don't believe this (well, mostly we don't believe it, even though China owns a huge proportion of the U.S. debt) is because of Adam Smith.

Trade Is a Win-Win

Trade, for Adam Smith, wasn't a zero-sum game. For a country to win, it wasn't necessary for another one to lose. Smith argued that trade benefits both countries. For example, suppose France was a more efficient producer of both brie and fighter jets than the United States, yet in the United States it was relatively cheaper to produce brie. If the United States specialized in brie and France specialized in fighter jets, both countries would fare better economically if they traded. That said, the fate of the West resting on France's fighter plane technology is about as frightening as American brie sold in individually wrapped slices.

So, trade is good, but just amassing more gold than the other guy—not so good. And here is where Adam Smith gets really interesting. Smith's whole philosophy of free-market economics and individual freedom rests on one very counterintuitive premise:

"Every individual . . . generally, indeed, neither intends to promote the public interest, nor knows how much he is promoting it. By preferring the support of domestic to that of foreign industry, he intends only his own security; and by directing that industry in such a manner as its produce may be of the greatest value, he intends only his own gain, and he is in this, as in many other cases, *led by an invisible hand* to promote an end which was no part of his intention."
[our emphasis]

In other words, everyone is basically selfish, but luckily being selfish indirectly benefits everyone else, all of whom are also selfish. Whew! And you were feeling guilty about getting that promotion while the rest of the country loses their jobs!

By people acting selfishly, Smith says, they can indirectly benefit society. Private vices, therefore, can actually generate public good. For Smith, a competitive free market generated by the rational self-interest of individuals would benefit everyone by keeping prices low while simultaneously incentivizing producers to make a wide variety of goods and services. So don't feel guilty about filling your own pockets, because as you do this you're unwittingly filling the coffers of us all. The mysterious force at work to make this all possible is what Smith famously called the "invisible hand," a phrase that's still very much in use by economists.

But this "invisible hand" isn't providing handouts. In Smith's capitalist economy, the more resourceful and ambitious you are, the more you make. As he gently puts it: "The real tragedy of the poor is the poverty of their aspirations."

> **"It is not from the benevolence of the butcher, the brewer, or the baker, that we can expect our dinner, but from their regard to their own interest."**
> —Adam Smith

That's right, so get off your ass and get serious, and don't rely on the state. In fact, Smith believed that efforts by the state to generate wealth were ineffectual compared to just letting the free market dictate the prices of goods and services. Smith saw his free-market capitalism as more than just a sound and effective economic framework for building wealth. He believed it was fundamental to the protection of individual freedom. The more the state lays off the economy, the less it intrudes into the affairs of individuals and the less power it has over the private lives of men. Smith's free-market capitalism is called "classical economics." A more extreme version of this theory is known as "laissez-faire" economics.

> **"It is not very unreasonable that the rich should contribute to the public expense, not only in proportion to their revenue, but something more than in that proportion."**
> —Adam Smith

ALEX KEATON'S FREE-MARKET MANIA

Now let's turn to one of the small screen's most enthusiastic exponents of free-market capitalism: Alex Keaton of the show *Family Ties*. The show ran on NBC from 1982 to 1989, smack in the middle of the Reagan years. Its premise was that Steven and Elyse Keaton, two liberals who married when they were young and participated in the Peace Corps and social movements for civil rights and against the Vietnam War, have a son, Alex, who's everything they're not. (They also have two daughters: Mallory, who's materialistic and self-absorbed; and Jennifer, probably the most normal of the three children.) A fourth child, Andrew, was introduced (and aged very rapidly) in the show's fifth season.

In any other era Alex Keaton would be an ideal son. He's smart, hard working, educated, respectful—a wet dream for most parents in any age. But this isn't any other age, and these aren't any other parents. Elyse and Steven Keaton were hippies, social progressives who came of age in the turbulent sixties in a counterculture that railed against the establishment and the cultural values that came with it. Elyse and Steven would rather catch their son hiding a garbage bag full of marijuana than a briefcase full of books by Adam Smith, Friedrich Hayek, and Milton Friedman. For the Keatons, times were a-changing once again, but this time the younger generation, personified by Alex Keaton, sought to re-establish the traditional values that their parent's generation had fought so violently to dismantle.

AUSTRIA MEETS CHICAGO
Friedrich Hayek (1899–1992) and Milton Friedman (1912–2006) were two of the most prominent defenders of classical free-market economic theory. Hayek's *The Road to Serfdom*, an important document of what's called the Austrian School of economics (because Hayek was Austrian—go figure!) was a blast against the kind of central planning advocated by Marxists. Friedman, a leader of the influential Chicago school of economists, was the most widely known advocate of laissez-faire theory.

Family Ties reflected the move in the United States away from the cultural liberalism of the 1960s and 1970s to the conservatism of the 1980s. It mapped this transition through the hysterical and heartfelt battles between Young Republican Alex Keaton and his ex-hippie parents.

A Pantheon of Conservatives

Most teenage boys idolize movie stars, comic book superheroes, and ball players. Their hobbies are sports, cars, and parties. Alex's heroes are the likes of Richard Nixon (the lunchbox Alex carries to high school has Nixon's picture on it), William F. Buckley Jr., and Ronald Reagan. While the other kids collect baseball cards, Alex gets his kicks by watching his favorite television show, *Wall $treet Week*, and by reading *The Wall Street Journal*. Yes, this was one peculiar teenage boy for one peculiar time.

As the show's creator, Gary David Goldberg, once asked: "When else could a boy with a briefcase become a national hero?"

There's no question, either, of Alex being portrayed as stupid or ignorant. On the contrary, he's far smarter than his sisters—particularly the vapid Mallory—and even, to an extent, his parents. He does well in school and is funny and clever in conversation.

In his Museum of Broadcast Communications entry for *Family Ties*, Michael Saenz argues that the show

> “. . . explored one of the intriguing cultural inversions characterizing the Reagan era: a conservative younger generation aspiring to wealth, business success, and traditional values, serves as inheritor to the politically liberal, presumably activist, culturally experimental generation of adults who had experienced the 1960s. The result was a decade . . . in which youthful ambition and social renovation became equated with pronounced political conservatism.”

THE GIPPER LOVES ALEX
Ronald Reagan once stated that *Family Ties* was his favorite television show.

The tension between these two philosophical divides, the consummate conservative capitalist, Alex Keaton, a poster boy for Adam Smith free-market principles, and his socially liberal, leftist-leaning ex-hippie parents, is the dominant theme throughout the series. The interaction of these two opposing philosophical viewpoints, this vast cultural divide, is what made the show dynamic and relevant—and, not to mention, funny.

Alex: How do I look?

Steven: Middle-aged.

Alex: Dad, recent studies show that you can predict success by the way a person dresses.

Steven: Alex, you're a young man. You shouldn't be worried about success. You should be thinking about hopping on a tramp steamer and going around the world, or putting a pack on your back and heading down to Mexico, South America, or anywhere.

Alex: The 1960s are over, Dad.

Steven: Thanks for the tip.

America in the eighties, like the Keaton family, was trying to find a way to fit these opposing pieces of its soul together. While Alex Keaton and, to some extent, his sister Mallory are conservative, their younger sister Jennifer, is a more feminist-leaning liberal like her mother. The Keatons, like America, were a family divided by political philosophy. And no one was too young to get in on the debate.

Andrew Keaton: Alex is reading me "Robin Hood," where he robs from the poor and gives to the rich.

Steven: That's not "Robin Hood," that's Ronald Reagan.

A Divided, But United, Family

Though they had differences, the Keatons, unlike many other families, were able to talk about them, even joke about them. It may be argued that this healthy debate actually served to bring them closer together. In the end, family trumps everything—whether Marx or Adam Smith.

For instance, when Alex is in an on-campus interview at Princeton University, Mallory barges into the interview room crying about her boyfriend kissing another girl. Alex, the driven future Wall Streeter, chooses to help his sister instead of completing the interview, ruining his shot at Princeton.

No matter what side of the philosophical divide you are on, the message goes, family is the most important thing.

(But Jesus Christ, Alex! The Ivy League! C'mon!)

CHAPTER 15
Dr. Gregory House and the Nietzschean Superman

"A casual stroll through the lunatic asylum shows that faith does not prove anything."
—Nietzsche

"What I have difficulty with is the whole concept of belief. Faith isn't based on logic or experience."
—Gregory House, MD

Friedrich Wilhelm Nietzsche (1844–1900) is one of the most controversial and misunderstood philosophers who ever lived. He's been accused of being responsible for the rise of Nazism, a precursor of totalitarian government, and any number of other wild things.

Nietzsche was born in Rocken, Germany. His father, a Lutheran pastor, died when the boy was only four years old and apparently had no influence on Nietzsche's development. By the time Nietzsche was twelve, the local schools knew he was a genius and sent him to Pforta, a renowned school in Germany. Following this, he enrolled in Bonn in the mid-1860s and by the age of just twenty-four began a teaching career at the university. After a prolific philosophical career, he suffered a mental breakdown in 1889, reportedly upon seeing a coachman cruelly whipping his horse. Nietzsche started to sob and threw his arms around the horse's neck (not exactly the image of the superman).

Nietzsche was a pessimist, in the tradition of Germans such as Arthur Schopenhauer (1788–1860). His philosophical conundrums were complicated by the fact that he suffered throughout his life from mental illness and died insane.

THE CHICAGO SUPERMEN

In 1924, two young men in Chicago, Nathan Leopold and Richard Loeb, were accused of murdering a young boy to see if they could get away with it. In the face of overwhelming evidence, they were found guilty, and the court met to consider sentence. Appearing for the defense to argue against the death penalty was the great criminal lawyer Clarence Darrow.

Darrow argued that Leopold and Loeb had committed the crime under the influence of Nietzsche's philosophy. "Is any blame attached," he asked, "because somebody took Nietzsche's philosophy seriously and fashioned his life upon it? . . . It is hardly fair to hang a 19-year-old boy for the philosophy that was taught him at the university."

The judge agreed, and Leopold and Loeb were sentenced to life imprisonment.

Nietzsche famously proclaimed that "God is dead." He meant by this that Christianity and the moral values it preached were obsolete, no longer applicable in modern life. More than that, Nietzsche saw traditional Christian morality as a harmful impediment to the progression of human freedom and achievement, both individual and collective. Just like the belief in God, the old moral values were outdated and needed to be replaced. Nietzsche preached the need for a new, more life-affirming moral code that celebrated excellence and strength rather than modesty and weakness, a new value structure reminiscent of the pre-Christian Greek and Roman moral values, which Nietzsche fondly called "noble morality." This new moral code would assist rather than hinder the individual to unleash his creative genius and reach his full potential. Who was to bring this new morality to the human race? Well, the superman of course!

"Whoever has overthrown an existing law of custom has always first been accounted a bad man . . . history treats almost exclusively of these bad men who subsequently became good men!"
—Nietzsche

PAGING DR. SUPERMAN

Dr. Gregory House is a super doctor, equipped with the uniquely ingenious capacity to diagnose diseases that other doctors cannot. Played by British actor Hugh Laurie, he's the star of *House*, which began running on Fox in 2004. House is the leader of a team of diagnosticians at a fictional hospital in New Jersey. Only those patients suffering from the most mysterious of medical maladies come to House for answers.

More often than not, he solves the mystery. Solves the puzzle. Bedside manner not being his forte, House makes no attempt to conceal the fact that it is the puzzle itself, not the actual suffering patient, that is his main interest.

> **"Treating illnesses is why we became doctors; treating patients is what makes most doctors miserable."**
> —Gregory House

And that's what we love about House: his hostile indifference to his patients. The only thing that rivals House's intelligence is his relentless rudeness to the patients, the staff, and everyone else he meets. So super doctor? Certainly. Super schmuck? Absolutely. But superman? Maybe. . . .

Nietzsche didn't envision the superman to be a human being. He didn't have enough faith in the current state of humanity to produce a superman.

> **"Man is a rope tied between beast and *Übermensch* [Superman]."**
> —Nietzsche

On the other hand, Nietzsche does write in other places that certain important personages in history stand out amongst the throng of everymen of their day. People like Jesus, Julius Caesar, Napoleon, and other bigshots might not be supermen, but they were definitely on the right track. Nietzsche believed that even the most mediocre society had value if it produced even one of these critical figures. According to this, even the existence of a place like New Jersey is defendable if it produces one extraordinary individual, such as Gregory House.

House may be human, but he is made to look as alien as possible in his environment. A casually dressed, pill popping, guitar playing, motorcycle-driving renegade, House's staunch individuality stands in contrast to the endlessly bureaucratic reality of hospital life. Gregory House, like Nietzsche's superman, marches to the beat of his own drum and follows his own rules. And everyone accepts this because, in the final analysis, House saves lives. Even his boss, hospital administrator Dr. Lisa Cuddy, whose ass is on the line every time House breaks the rules, admits it: "He saves more lives than he loses," she says.

House is seen as special by everyone at the hospital and is therefore held to a different standard. No other doctor could continuously thwart the hospital rules and procedural policies, putting the patient's life in danger and the hospital in danger of a lawsuit, but House can. He can because there is a general recognition of his brilliance, a recognition that House does not have to play by the same rules as everyone else because he is not the same as everyone else. He is different, more evolved in some way. There are house rules that everyone must abide by, and then there are rules for House.

HOUSE TO RESCUE HUMANITY

Nietzsche's superman ideal has to be more than just a quick-witted medical genius with a penchant for breaking rules; he has to help usher in an entirely new moral conception for humanity to embrace. A new moral character. A new moral ideal. A new way of looking at the world.

House teaches his staff more than just medical know-how. He offers his wide-eyed disciples lessons about the nature of the human character that are critical to solving the medical mystery. Like Sherlock Holmes, House does not disregard even the most seemingly innocuous fact. Nothing is taken for granted, most especially the patient's word. House's dictum, "Everybody lies," may just sound cynical, but this unfortunate truth must be accepted if you are to solve the medical case—and save the life. He constantly urges his staff to "overcome" their traditional medical education to get the job done and save the life at hand. He urges them to break into patients' homes, reject the advice of superiors, and do a slew of other things that could get them into serious trouble. To throw off the shackles of Western medical dogma and bureaucratic limitations and replace them with a new, more dynamic set of values—this is what draws young doctors to study with Gregory House. House even coerces his staff to confront their own moral concepts and beliefs, insisting, like Nietzsche, that the old moral framework no longer applies.

In one episode, when House finds out that one of the young doctors, Dr. Jeffrey Cole, is a Mormon, he insists that it be he who performs a unique experiment of drinking tequila with the patient to see the difference in how her liver will react. When Dr. Cole declines, House brings out his razor-sharp wit: "Would you pull an ass out of a pit on the Sabbath?" he asks, referring to Jesus' statement that the Sabbath was made for man, rather than man being made for the Sabbath. Jesus' point was that it was okay to do work or good deeds even when they conflict with commandments.

In typical fashion, House later asked the young doctor why he betrayed his religious beliefs. "You make a good argument," Cole answers.

Yes, as with any good philosopher, that's the doc's specialty.

BUT WHAT ABOUT CLARK KENT?

If Nietzsche was writing about a superman in the late nineteenth century, did Joe Shuster and Jerry Siegel have this in mind when they created Superman for Detective Comics (later DC Comics) in 1938? Possibly, although they would have denied that Superman had many of the typical Nietzschean characteristics. But what about his television incarnation?

We'll leave aside *The Adventures of Superman*, which ran from 1952 to 1958 and starred George Reeves, and *Lois and Clark*, starring Dean Cain and Teri Hatcher, which aired on NBC from 1993 to 1997. Neither of these shows really dealt very much with the moral dilemmas faced by a guy with super powers from Krypton. But what about *Smallville*, starring Tom Welling, which began on the WB Network in 2001?

THE DEATH OF SUPERMAN

George Reeves, who played Superman in the 1950s, was an unassuming workhorse actor. Superman was probably his biggest role. (He can be glimpsed briefly in an early scene of *Gone with the Wind*; he also sang on the *Tony Bennett Show* and appeared in an episode of *I Love Lucy*.) On June 16, 1959, he died of a gunshot wound to the head. The official verdict was suicide, but many investigators since then have suggested it was murder. The death was the subject of the film *Hollywoodland*, starring Ben Affleck.

Because that show has run for ten years, the writers have had a lot of time to have Clark Kent/Superboy think about his choices. The basic paradox of the show has been that Clark wants to be normal, even as it becomes more and more clear that he'll have to make decisions and take actions that will affect millions of people all over the globe. Superman doesn't want to be a superman, but he may not have a choice. A Nietzschean problem indeed!

But if Clark rejects Nietzsche's *Übermensch*, the series does contain someone who embraces it: Lex Luthor, played by Michael Rosenbaum. The odd friendship between Clark and Lex that was featured in the early part of the series gradually came apart (as it had to, of course, if the writers were going to stay true to the comic books), and Lex was revealed as a power-hungry corporate mogul. Lex sees himself as superior to everyone, by virtue of both his money and his intelligence, as well as by virtue of his willingness to do things no one else will. He's perfectly willing to destroy individual lives in pursuit of what he believes, in his twisted way, to be the greater good.

[Lex points to a breastplate with an "S" symbol.]

Lex: You know it belonged to Alexander the Great? They said the design symbolizes strength and courage.

Clark: I can't exactly see myself going into battle with that on my chest.

Lex: Darker times call for darker methods. His opponents thought he was invincible.

Clark: I didn't know you were such a history buff.

Lex: I'm not. I'm just interested in people who ruled the world before they were thirty.

He and Gregory House, should they ever meet, will have a lot to talk about.

Lex Luthor left the show after seven seasons. We assume he's somewhere out there, plotting a Nietzschean takeover of the world.

PITY ME? SCREW YOU!

Let's get back to *House*. Another element to the internal chaos that is Dr. Gregory House is his absolute lack of self-pity and resentment. Although he suffers from a leg infarction that forces him to walk with a cane, he doesn't look with envy on those who can run like the wind as he limps behind. He never tries to force anyone's empathy. We feel bad for House, for his physical pain and his consequent addiction to Vicodin, but he never asks us—or anyone else—to do so. For his mental and physical toughness and lack of self-pity, Nietzsche would give House a big thumbs-up.

Nietzsche believed that Judeo-Christian morality, or "slave morality," came into being out of the resentment of the weak over the strong. In their brilliant wickedness, the pioneers of this moral framework toppled the more noble morality embraced in antiquity by the ancient Greeks and Romans, a morality, like the kind Aristotle described, that understood the virtuous man to be a man who is a master of excellence, rather than the Christian idea of a virtuous man being one who follows the commands of a God with slavelike obedience. He called these two opposing moralities "master" and "slave" morality, respectively. Man should be a master of his destiny, not a slave to it.

With a contemptuous disgust for this kind of "resentment," which brought slave morality to the world, the Nietzschean superman must thrive in almost a stoic fashion regardless of what plagues him, without expressing an ounce of self-pity, not a drop of resentment.

> **"I take risks, sometimes patients die, but not taking risks causes more patients to die—so I guess my biggest problem is I've been cursed with the ability to do the math."**
>
> —Dr. Gregory House

For those who are willing to listen, House may indeed have moral lessons that could help usher in a new moral consciousness, the kind that Nietzsche was hoping for. House, like the superman, is a moral renegade, rejecting the moral framework that surrounds him and living life by his own rules, rules that more often than not save lives. While House might be far more of a snarky prick than Nietzsche envisioned his superman to be, he is the closest thing—on screen and off—that we have to a man who has the charisma, the intelligence, and the moral courage to usher in a new era of moral thinking. Plus, let's face it, he's just cool.

THE SELF-HATING CHRISTIAN

Nietzsche thought Christian morality was the result of the natural aggressive impulse of man turned inward. Consider the priest or monk who denies himself (hopefully!) the pleasures of the flesh. His denial, far from being "noble," is really just his natural aggressive impulse directed at himself. The Judeo-Christian concept of "original sin"—that man must be redeemed—which as we saw came into Western thought with our old friend Augustine, is a perverse concept that led to a guilt-ridden conscious that has stifled man's spiritual advancement. This is why Nietzsche favors a more "life-affirming" or "man-affirming" morality, a noble one that allows us to express our natural aggressive impulses and affirm, rather than deny, our mental and physical needs. For Nietzsche, man's mission was self-mastery, self-assertion, and the creation of his own values, not the so-called "humility" of turning the other cheek or the "modesty" of denying the expression of our natural instincts. Nietzsche once referred to himself as the "most terrible opponent of Christianity." Now *that's* punk rock.

CHAPTER 16

Don Draper, George Costanza, and the Non-Meaning of Life

> "Life can only be understood backwards;
> but it must be lived forwards."
> —Søren Kierkegaard

> "It's your life. You don't know how long it's gonna last, but you know it doesn't end well. You've gotta move forward . . . as soon as you can figure out what that means."
> —Don Draper

Existence trumps essence. This is the core principle of Existentialism. Life may have no meaning, but that's no reason to fret. You exist, you are alive, and that is all that matters—and you should make the most of it. You as an individual have the power to reinvent yourself.

Søren Kierkegaard, the father of Existentialism, rejected the popular Hegelian philosophy of his day, which viewed individuals as faceless pawns in an unrelenting unfolding of history. "What about me?" whined Kierkegaard. "I don't care if history is marching toward some rational goal, I am the one that feels like shit when it rains." So Kierkegaard pulled philosophy down from the purview of Hegel's Absolute Spirit to the meaningless existence of the individual.

Kierkegaard (1813–1855) was Danish, which might account for the gloomy character of his philosophical approach (remember that Hamlet in Shakespeare is called "the melancholy Dane"). He was born in Copenhagen to a rich family, the youngest of seven children. Kierkegaard went to all the best schools, had his roomed cleaned by maids, and spent his time brooding over the emptiness of Hegelian philosophy—and of life itself. Despite his passionate writings, he himself lived a relatively uneventful life. After a long love affair with books, he became engaged to Regine Olsen. He broke the engagement soon thereafter, however, believing that domestic responsibility would hinder him in his philosophical calling.

He took an ironic approach in his writing, so sometimes it's difficult to know when he's being serious and when he's pulling our leg. At times, he's like Lt. Columbo from the TV show *Columbo*, which starred Peter Falk and ran from 1971 to 1978 on NBC. Columbo was apparently a bumbling idiot, always losing things, seemingly only half aware of his surroundings, chewing perpetually on what appeared to be the same damn cigar through the show's run. But whenever he was closing in on a criminal, who'd been lulled into a false sense of security by Columbo's antics—*snap!*—the trap would close, and the perpetrator was hauled off to jail.

That's what Kierkegaard is like. He wants to come off as an eccentric to conceal the sharpness of his mind.

THE MEANING OF LIFE

For the philosophers who preceded Kierkegaard, the universe is a meaningful place. Aristotle argued that everything that exists had a purpose, or *telos*. The purpose of an acorn is to become a tree. The purpose of an apple seed is to become an apple. For Hegel, you may remember, human history itself had a *telos*, which he saw as the progression of ultimate freedom toward Absolute Spirit.

But for Kierkegaard and his fellow existentialists, there is no inherent purpose in the universe, no objective meaning to our lives. It is up to us then to make our experience count, up to us as individuals to give our life meaning.

> **"I see it all perfectly; there are two possible situations—one can either do this or that. My honest opinion and my friendly advice is this: do it or do not do it—you will regret both."**
> —Søren Kierkegaard

How? Well, that depends on the existentialist. The novelist and existentialist Albert Camus (1913–1960) recommends that we "live to the point of tears." Jean-Paul Sartre (1905–1980), one of the most famous of all existentialist philosophers, advises, "Life begins on the other side of despair." Friedrich Nietzsche warns that "if you gaze too long into the abyss, the abyss will gaze back into you." (Yes, we know Nietzsche wasn't an existentialist, but it's a really cool quotation.)

Kierkegaard himself tells us to find a truth and live that truth "passionate and sincerely" and to do our best to deal with despair, a despair that comes from the understanding of the absurdity and meaninglessness of our existence. For a character like *Mad Men*'s Don Draper, a three-martini lunch might not be the answer, but it does make despair more tolerable.

DON DRAPER: EXISTENTIAL ANGST NEVER LOOKED SO GOOD

Mad Men is a genuine phenomenon. Premiering in 2007 on AMC, it's drawn a huge viewing audience, and there's even been a revival of some of the fashions popular among advertising executives in the 1960s. It's set in New York at the Sterling Cooper ad agency, and it stars Jon Hamm as the charismatic Don Draper, creative director of the agency.

EXISTENTIALISM BRINGS IN GOLD
In its first three seasons, *Mad Men* won thirteen Emmys and four Golden Globes.

It so happens we know quite a bit about the character of Don Draper. He was born in Illinois to a twenty-two-year-old prostitute who died giving birth to him; his real name is Richard Whitman. He was raised by his biological father, Archibald "Archie" Whitman, and stepmother, Abigail. Years later, Draper served in the Korean

War, where he switched identities with a fellow soldier who was killed next to him. After a stint as a used car salesman he found his way to New York City, where he went to City College, met his hot wife, Betty Draper, and eventually secured a job at Sterling Cooper advertising agency. He is married to Betty Draper, with whom he has three kids. He drinks, smokes, and screws everything that walks.

Don Draper, the coolest cat to grace the small or the big screen in decades, is the James Bond of the advertising world, the slick, handsome charmer who always gets the girl. But unlike 007, Draper is not only capable of moments of anxiety and angst, he's tortured by them.

JEAN-PAUL SARTRE: THE EXISTENTIALIST'S EXISTENTIALIST

Sartre was a philosopher (author of such unreadable books as *Being and Nothingness*), a poet, a playwright, a novelist, and a political activist. You have to wonder when he found time to form a romantic relationship with the feminist writer Simone de Beauvoir. Even though he's best known as an existentialist, he flirted with Marxism for a while and went so far as to join the French Communist Party. Nothing really came of it, and his attempts to reconcile Marxism with Existentialism embarrassed everybody involved.

Behind the exquisitely tailored suit and the perfectly combed hair, Draper suffers. Not from lack of love or lack of money or lack of sex; in fact, this enviable character seems to have it all. But what does this seemingly perfect life amount to in a world without meaning? Dashing Don suffers from a kind of existential dread that even the most exciting blissful indiscretion can't cure—and not for lack of trying!

For Draper, there is no grand plan. The universe is cold, indifferent, valueless.

> **"You're born alone and you die alone and this world just drops a bunch of rules on top of you to make you forget those facts. But I never forget. I'm living like there's no tomorrow, because there isn't one."**
>
> **—Don Draper**

So it's up to him to carve out some meaning, some reason for living, on his own. It's a journey of self-actualization fueled by booze, sex, and—surprise, surprise!—books.

Take *Exodus*, Leon Uris's epic novel about the founding of the state of Israel. Don first reads the book as homework in his pursuit of his first Jewish client, the sexy, savvy Rachel Menken. Like the heroes of *Exodus*, Draper does not allow his own tormented history to keep him from redefining himself, and moving forward to create his own destiny. If there is no land of milk and honey, then . . . build one. Imagine one. Create one.

The Existentialist City of Angels

Don's own personal exodus eventually leads him to California, where he immerses himself in a world of freethinking bohemian hedonists who break free of the shackles of modern morality and social norms. Like all good existentialists, Draper loves L.A.: "Everything is new, and it's clean, and the people are filled with hope."

Los Angeles is a city without a past, the perfect place for a man who has left his own past behind him. Los Angeles, like Draper, marches ceaselessly into the future—in stark contrast to New York, which Draper calls "a city in decay."

In L.A. Don considers leaving his family, his job, and his life back East for a carefree life drenched in sun. But he proves too spiritually evolved to retire to a life of pure pleasure. More's the pity—at least according to his pleasure-seeking pal Roger Sterling.

WILL THE REAL DON DRAPER PLEASE STAND UP?

True to existentialist philosophy, Don Draper has no essence. Just like California, there is no "there" there. But if you think that means that Draper is inauthentic and amoral, a shallow salesman without a soul, think again. Sartre and Kierkegaard would fight you on that.

> "A man who as a physical being is always turned toward the outside, thinking that his happiness lies outside him, finally turns inward and discovers that the source is within him."
> —Søren Kierkegaard

From the existentialist point of view, as long as Draper chooses what he does freely and accepts responsibility for what he does, then he is both authentic and moral. Consider this scenario:

Should Don Draper screw the hot chick or not?

This is a trick question: Whether Don screws her or not is not the issue. What matters is whether he chooses freely, either way—and then takes full responsibility for his choice. As an existentialist, Draper would never say: "I will not screw that hot chick because I am married and my marriage vows forbid it." His marriage vows are irrelevant; what matters is whether he chooses to honor them. Or not.

For Draper, it's mostly not. Which makes him the baddest existentialist TV hero in recent memory.

GEORGE COSTANZA: MASTER OF HIS OWN EXISTENTIAL DOMAIN

Now let's turn to another existential hero—one in every way the opposite of Draper, at least on the surface. If *Seinfeld* is a show about nothing, then George Costanza is the court jester of nothing.

> **"I lie every second of the day. My whole life is a sham."**
> —George Costanza

George Costanza is a half-Italian, half-Jewish, fully neurotic, not-so-proud son of the eternally squabbling Frank and Estelle Costanza. He sees his trademark neurosis, deceitfulness, insecurity, and lack of ambition—the basic elements of his personality—as the result of his parents staying together rather than splitting up. Interestingly, the character was originally based on *Seinfeld* co-creator Larry David, but surnamed after Jerry Seinfeld's real-life New York friend, Mike Costanza.

When Larry David and Jerry Seinfeld created *Seinfeld*, they had two rules:

1. No hugging
2. No learning

We weren't supposed to learn any moral lessons from watching *Seinfeld* and we weren't supposed to care much about the characters either. This may seem like a pretty nihilist formula for a show, but hey, who can argue with success?

In a purposeless world, Albert Camus may prefer we live to the point of tears, but Larry David would rather we laugh our ass off. And that's exactly what George, Jerry, Elaine, and Kramer make us do: They make us laugh.

> **"Every existing thing is born without reason, prolongs itself out of weakness, and dies by chance."**
> —Jean-Paul Sartre

Even death is funny in *Seinfeld*. Who can forget the episode when George's fiancée dies from licking all those wedding invitations made with toxic glue that George bought her? His bride-to-be dies and we can't stop laughing, all the harder when we realize how relieved George is at her untimely demise.

Fake It 'Til You Make It

George the existentialist can choose to be who he wants to be. No one takes advantage of the existentialist's lack of absolute truth more than he does. For George, truth is subjective. As George tells Jerry when he asks him how to pass a polygraph test: "Just remember, Jerry. It isn't a lie if you believe it."

When George believes his own lies, he can become the kind of person he wants to be. In one of the funniest and most memorable episodes in the history of television, George lies to impress a cute girl he knew in high school. He tells her that he is a marine biologist—and he's promptly put to the test. He takes a walk on the beach with this girl, and they come across a crowd of people watching a whale drown. The call goes out for a marine biologist—and George must either roll up his sleeves and save the day or be exposed as a charlatan. So off to the sea he waddles in search of himself—and when he finds himself, he's a marine biologist!

No Exit from Seinfeld's World

> "Hell is other people."
> —Jean-Paul Sartre

The *Seinfeld* characters are anything but compassionate. Indeed, in the series finale they are accused of criminal negligence, and put on trial for breaking the "Good Samaritan" law. Witnesses wronged by the *Seinfeld* gang in previous episodes show up to testify against them. This is one callous and selfish group of pals, they claim. In the end, George and his pals continue the same empty conversations about nothing that they've been having for years.

It is no mistake that the series ends much the same way it began, with these so-called friends bored, miserable, and alienated. We first meet George and company in an empty parking lot, we leave them in a jail cell, but it really doesn't matter where you are. You are stuck with yourself and your existential woe wherever you go.

George, Jerry, Elaine, and Kramer are friends more out of convenience than true compassion and love for one another. After all, if you're going to be doomed to live in a meaningless world, you might as well shoot the shit with like-minded narcissists and have a couple of laughs—in jail or out.

> **"I relate to George through you.
> We're more like friends-in-law."**
> —Elaine to Jerry, *Seinfeld*

It's a scene right out of a Sartre play. No, really. In the great existentialist's one-act *No Exit*, the characters are forced to spend eternity in one room, with only their sorry selves to keep them company. Its theme is one George Costanza and Larry David could relate to: Hell is other people.

CHAPTER 17

Jersey Shore's "The Situation": The Randian Ideal Man with a Tan?

> "[Objectivism] is the concept of man as a heroic being, with his own happiness as the moral purpose of his life, with productive achievement as his noblest activity, and reason as his only absolute."
>
> —Ayn Rand

> "With me and Sammi, it's not a matter of if she wants to hook up with me; it's a matter of just when I decide."
>
> —Mike "The Situation" Sorrentino

Ayn Rand (1905–1982) was an American novelist and philosopher, famous for the novels *The Fountainhead* and *Atlas Shrugged*. Her philosophy is called *objectivism*. She put reason before emotion and individualism over groupthink; she thought egotism was a good thing and altruism was a negative character trait. Needless to say, she was no stranger to controversy.

Perhaps the reason Rand developed her philosophy was the circumstances of her youth. She was a child in Russia in the tumultuous days of the Bolshevik Revolution of 1917. She came to the United States in 1926 to seek her fortune and to be able to express her thoughts and beliefs freely and without fear of persecution. Such freedoms that we take for granted were not to be found in the former Soviet Union. In fact, her first novels, *Anthem* and *We the Living*, are cautionary tales set in what are called *dystopias*. Just as the word *utopia* means a perfect paradise, a dystopia is the reverse, a repressive totalitarian state. George Orwell's *1984* is the most famous example of this literary trope.

Rand believed in the ultimate heroism of man, and that mankind's goal is to achieve great success, with each individual fulfilling his and her human potential to the max, and this self-interest superseding the needs of the needy collective. Individual accomplishment is what makes society great. Food stamps and the welfare state are not in the objectivist playbook.

Mankind is the ultimate in the cosmos, so say the objectivists. No gods, angels, or demons. There is no Prime Mover in the Aristotelian tradition. Man is the Prime Mover and is the end, not the means to anything or anyone else.

Rand set out her philosophy in the novels *The Fountainhead* (1943) and her most important novel, *Atlas Shrugged*, published in 1957. The theme of *Atlas Shrugged* is the conflict between the individual creative spirit embodied in the heads of great industries throughout the United States, and a powerful state apparatus that seeks to control the lives of its citizens in some dystopic future. As people come increasingly under the control of a vast, powerful national government structure, more and more people pick up on a catch phrase being bandied about: Who is John Galt? The question doesn't seem to have any meaning at first, beyond a cynical, "Don't ask difficult questions because we don't have the answers." However, by the end of the novel it's clear that John Galt is the leader of a secret band of industrial leaders. These leaders have organized a massive strike against the government, withdrawing from their companies and leaving them to wither and die. Faced with this, the national government begins to collapse, and Galt and his fellow industrialists emerge as the force that will organize a new order based on individual creativity and autonomy from the state.

ALMOST AS POPULAR AS GOD

Rand's books have sold over 25 million copies, selling more than 800,000 each year, according to the Ayn Rand Institute. In 1991, when the Book of the Month Club asked club members what book most influenced their lives, Rand's *Atlas Shrugged* placed second only to the Bible. If that statistic doesn't reflect the odd and arguably contradictory nature of the American psyche, we don't know what does.

WHAT'S IN IT FOR ME?

Most moral philosophical theories focus on either the outcomes of action (i.e., if the action follows some moral rule like "killing is wrong") or the character of the act (i.e., if the intention of the actor is good). However, Rand—like Aristotle, from whom she drew influence— focuses on the character of the actor himself. This is called *virtue ethics*.

Rand, in her depiction of the ideal man, such as John Galt, believes a moral act is one that stems from the ideal man's rational desire to promote his own happiness. The basic tool the Randian man uses to obtain the highest moral value (his own happiness) is the exercise of Reason.

> **"From the smallest necessity to the highest religious abstraction, from the wheel to the skyscraper, everything we are and everything we have comes from one attribute of man—the function of his reasoning mind."**
> —Ayn Rand

So, to be an ideal chap in Rand's book, you have to use your capacity for reason to live life for yourself, not for others.

The Randian hero exemplifies ethical egoism, the normative ethical position that the self-interest of the individual ought to be the basis for moral action. "[Man] . . . must exist for his own sake, neither sacrificing himself to others nor sacrificing others to himself."

And who lives for himself more than the great Mike "The Situation" Sorrentino of *Jersey Shore*? As he says: "I ran the house . . . I did whatever I wanted, I took whatever I wanted, and it was my world."

Who Is "The Situation"?

"Who is John Galt?" This is the central question consistently raised in Rand's *Atlas Shrugged*, not only, as we've seen, as a rhetorical inquiry, but increasingly throughout the book as a philosophic dilemma and finally as a call to revolution against socialism. The novel depicts the world in which John Galt tries to thrive as a stifling, egalitarian nightmare where mediocrity reigns. Who is John Galt? John Galt is the

Randian hero, the ultimate symbol of individual excellence and the moral rightness of self-interested action over altruism and sacrifice.

> "Civilization is the progress toward a society of privacy. The savage's whole existence is public, ruled by the laws of his tribe. Civilization is the process of setting man free from men."
> —Ayn Rand

Out of all the galloping guidos who have stolen our hearts on *Jersey Shore*, Michael Sorrentino stands above the others. Nicknamed simply "The Situation" because, you know, he's like a situation, Sorrentino is the embodiment of modern masculinity. He is, in fact, a new ideal man, at least from Rand's perspective.

Sorrentino grew up in Manalapan, New Jersey. He went on to work as an assistant manager of a fitness center in Staten Island and, when he was twenty-five, began underwear modeling. In 2009, he and seven other young people began their odyssey on MTV's *Jersey Shore*. In 2010, the cast of the show was named to Barbara Walters's 10 Most Fascinating People list—some people's idea of fame.

EVERYBODY LOVES SNOOKI—ALMOST

During the filming of *The Jersey Shore*, Nicole "Snooki" Polizzi was punched in the face during a bar fight in Seaside Heights, New Jersey. Her appearance fees immediately shot up from $2,000 to $10,000.

Now, there are some obvious differences between John Galt and The Situation. For one, Galt is from Ohio and The Situation is from

Staten Island, though both places register equally low as world tourist destinations. Also, Galt is more educated than The Situation. Galt went to college and studied philosophy, while The Situation is more of a self-educated man, kind of like Abraham Lincoln with more abs and less brains. But, like Galt, The Situation has risen from blue-collar beginnings to make a major impact on our culture. Both men have used whatever rationality they possess (admittedly, in The Situation's case, not much) to make the self-interested choices that will lead to the promotion of their own happiness.

THE GUIDO GUIDEBOOK

The guidos of *Jersey Shore* live their life by a strict code: GTL. An acronym for "gym, tan, laundry," GTL is the core ethical foundation of the guido, his guide to navigating the cruel and indifferent world. It is this undying devotion to GTL that gets every guido up every morning to brave another difficult day of drinking, fist-pumping, and grenade dodging. It is their purpose. Their reason for living. And we are lucky . . . nay, we are blessed to be allowed even a glimpse into the fascinating, esoteric world of the Jersey Shore. Here is the Guido Code explained by Pauly D: "I was born and raised a guido. It's just a lifestyle. It's being Italian, it's representing family, friends, tanning, gel . . . everything."

Fascinating, isn't it?

For John Galt this happiness meant a restructuring of the political framework from socialistic statism to a freer, capitalistic society in which the ideal man can thrive and move forward, instead of stagnating. As for The Situation, you don't go from being an assistant manager of a gym in Staten Island to a superstar making $5 million a year, not to mention appearing on *Dancing with the Stars*, through acts of altruism. Happiness for The Situation might be something less grandiose than for Galt, like driving a brand-new Bentley to the bank while having his shirt off. Either way, both these men value, celebrate, and promote their own happiness above all else. Rand's assumption is that the enlightened self-interest of each person will collectively lead to a freer, happier society.

The Situation exercises Galt's heroic attitude toward life, the attitudinal absolute that Rand requires of her ideal man. In this respect, he's even more Randian than John Galt. We never saw John Galt without his shirt, did we? And I'll bet if he'd ever taken it off, there's no way *his* body would resemble a tanned Greek god. And who has the cooler name? John Galt is okay, but . . . *The Situation*? If that's not the best name for an ideal man-god, we don't know what is.

THE ORIGIN OF "THE SITUATION"
According to Sitch, one day on Miami Beach a girl ordered her boyfriend to look at Mike's chiseled abs. A friend then turned to him and said, "Mike, that's a situation right there." Hence, The Situation. Mike Sorrentino's request to trademark "The Situation" for a line of T-shirts and underwear was denied by the U.S. trademark office. Is there no justice in this world?

Finally, a Randian for Our Times

As an atheist who thought faith incompatible with reason, Rand rejected religion, mysticism, or supernaturalism of any kind.

Nonetheless, she encouraged a peculiar kind of personality cult around her. Her Objectivist disciples formed a group in the 1950s named the Collective. The name was chosen ironically, since they were, in fact, staunch individualists. The group consisted of future big-shots like Nathaniel Branden, a prominent psychotherapist; his then-wife Barbara Branden, later a well-known editor and writer; Alan Greenspan, future head of the Federal Reserve; and Leonard Peikoff, a Canadian philosopher and continuing exponent of Rand's thought. Think of the Collective as Andy Warhol's circle at The Factory only without all the drugs and sex and . . . well, fun.

Or think of it as *Jersey Shore*, only with brains.

AMERICAN IDOL AND THE RANDIAN IDEAL

Given the narcissistic character of much of current American society, you'd think television would be awash in Rand-inspired characters. But when we start to look more closely at the current TV scene, we find that really isn't so. Almost all shows tend to depict characters who either act in concert with society (for instance, Sam Waterston's Jack McCoy on *Law & Order*, who acts as an instrument of the state in pursuing justice) or characters who appear as self-interested individuals but underneath are willing to help their fellow men and women. A character of this type is Ted Danson's Dr. Becker in the show of the same name. Becker is a grouch and a misanthrope, but he cares enough about his patients to sacrifice his career to work in a low-income neighborhood among people who really need his services.

Still, there is one show that's very much based on the notion of self-interest leading to a successful outcome: *American Idol*.

First, a few words about this show. It's one of the most brilliant concepts in American television in some time. It was an American version of the British show *Pop Idol*, created by Simon Fuller, an enterprising Brit. It started in 2002 and almost immediately riveted the American public. Its huge ratings made Fox TV a major player among the American networks. Contest winners and runners-up have sold tens of millions of albums, accounting for more than 2 percent of total U.S. music sales. Some contestants, such as Clay Aiken and Jennifer Hudson, have gone on to have careers on Broadway or in film. Some, albeit not that many, have actually become significant music stars.

From the studios' standpoint, *American Idol* has crowdsourced the talent and audition process, allowing the American public to participate in the process of selecting recording talent and giving them a vested interest in the success of the artists they choose (we're using the word *artist* in a loose sense here, considering some of the people who've succeeded on *American Idol*).

What does this all have to do with Ayn Rand?

Simple. This is the process Rand had in mind when she wrote *Atlas Shrugged*. The most creative, talented people are forced to the top by the relentless pressure of competition. They can't be selected blindly by the state (or, in the case of *Idol*, by the record companies). The very process of capitalist-driven competition, fueled by self-interest, brings true talent to the fore.

Consider the auditions for *Idol*. Thousands upon thousands of people show up at each stop of the *Idol* judges' tour. They're not interested, for the most part, in helping each other or serving the music industry gods. They want to make it to the top. They're in it for themselves. In other words, they act from pure self-interest, without any attempt to subsume themselves to larger corporate-driven goals.

As they move up the mighty ziggurat of the show's auditions—before a panel of selectors, then a group of producers, then the judges, and then, if they're lucky, on to Hollywood and yet another round of auditions and cuts—slowly the less talented are winnowed away. Finally, what we're left with is the fifteen or so most talented of all those hundreds of thousands of people we started with.

And those people provide entertainment that keep the rest of us happy and send us off to work singing along with the latest Kelly Clarkson hit or Carrie Underwood song or, we suppose in some forgotten backwater, Taylor Hicks.

The Randian system benefits both the individual *and* society. Rand sees selfishness as a virtue that should be encouraged. She would have enjoyed the character of Gordon Gekko in the movie *Wall Street*, with his creed: "Greed . . . is good."

CHAPTER 18

Earl Hickey Meets Karma in My Name Is Earl

"For every event that occurs, there will follow another event whose existence was caused by the first, and this second event will be pleasant or unpleasant according as its cause was skillful or unskillful."
—The Buddha

"Karma is a funny thing."
—Earl J. Hickey

"Karma's a bitch." It's an expression you have heard throughout your life. But is it true? Certainly if you treat everyone badly, chances are you won't be the most popular guy on the block, but that is a far philosophical cry from the theory that there is a metaphysical moral force in the universe that rewards the good, and punishes the wicked.

For a Buddhist, Buddha's moral law of karma is just as real and fundamental as Newton's laws of physics. Do evil and the universe ensures that evil is done unto you. Likewise, be good to others and good things shall come to you. Sounds nice, but what about all the good people who suffer evil? The starving child, the crime victim, the congressman's wife. How is it that good people suffer these indignities if the universe is inherently moral and just?

THIS AIN'T YOUR FIRST RODEO

Past lives. Reincarnation. That's the answer that karma offers. It may seem as though the infant born with AIDS is an innocent victim of cruel random indifference, but in reality his suffering is not random at all. Rather, he is suffering because of the evil deeds he committed in a past life. This means that even if someone is evil in this life, he will pay for his sins in another. So if you know a bad person who basks in prosperity and happiness, don't worry. Eventually, the Buddha says, he will get his due.

EASTERN RELIGION *IS* EASTERN PHILOSOPHY

Who exactly was the Buddha? He was an Indian prince, Siddhartha Gautama (ca. 563–ca. 483 B.C.). He was extremely wealthy, but in his youth he had a revelation that his wealth was meaningless. Realizing that the world was filled with poverty, disease, and suffering, he rejected his wealthy lifestyle and sought spiritual enlightenment instead. At last, after a prolonged meditation, he came to the conclusion that our understanding of the world can be reduced to what he called the Four Noble Truths.

The Four Noble Truths

Like Jesus, Buddha never committed anything to paper. As a result, it was his followers who chronicled his life and philosophy. The core of Buddhism centers on what are called the Four Noble Truths.

The truth is not always what you want to hear, but the truth shall set ye free. The **first Noble Truth** is that life is inherently sad and full of suffering. Birth is a painful process and so is death, and in between are affliction, heartbreak, the death of loved ones, and your own inexorable trot toward your inevitable demise. Nobody gets out of here alive. And because Buddhists believe in reincarnation, you don't even get your wings when it's over. You get to do it all over again in another life.

The **second Noble Truth** explains why we suffer. It is because people are unenlightened and unaware of the true nature of the universe. This and our obsession with earthly desires and material things add to life's endemic melancholy. Most people are mired in the world of sensual pleasures and creature comforts; yet while such things may provide transient gratification, they thwart true enlightenment.

The **third Noble Truth** is an optimistic one. You can transcend your earthly woes by shaking off the shackles of materialism and other sensual indulgences and seeking enlightenment. Meditation is the path for most Buddhists. In this age of decreasing attention spans, meditation is a tall order. You cannot fiddle with your Sony PlayStation while waiting for the Great Awakening. For the newbie, meditation is difficult work. Most people get antsy waiting in line for a movie or at the bank, let alone sitting with legs crossed, concentrating on their breathing and waiting for something to happen.

The **fourth and final Noble Truth** is that by following the Eightfold Path of Enlightenment, you can find the bliss that we all seek. (More on that in a minute.)

Eastern philosophers like the Buddha and the early Hindu scholars did not feel compelled to offer a logical justification or argument to prove the validity of their theories in the same scientific fashion of their Western counterparts. There is a fine line between Eastern religion and Eastern philosophy, whereas the line in the West is clear. Philosophy is based on the use of Reason, religion on faith. The Hindu and Buddhist scholars make no real attempt to show empirical evidence of the existence of karma and reincarnation, at least not to the extent that a Western philosopher approaches moral theory.

Regardless of the different methodology, the purpose of karma is to persuade people to right action. Action is key here, as the word *karma* translates as "action."

WALK THE EARTH LIKE CAINE

Television hasn't had a lot of Buddhist heroes, but the most well known is probably the character Kwai Chang Caine from the show *Kung Fu*. The show ran from 1972 to 1975 and starred David Carradine as Caine. *Kung Fu* was sort of a Western—Caine was traveling through the Old West, searching for his brother, Danny Caine—but it was heavily imbued with Eastern spiritualism.

CARRADINE OR BRUCE

The great martial artist and actor Bruce Lee was considered for the part of Caine but was rejected in favor of David Carradine. Lee went back to Hong Kong and began making action films that were the foundation of a very lucrative career, which ended in 1973 with Lee's death. In 1986, Carradine made *Kung Fu: The Movie*, in which he fights his son, Chung Wang. Ironically, Chung Wang was played by Brandon Lee, son of Bruce Lee.

Throughout the series, Caine remembers the Buddhist wisdom that was instilled in him in his youth by his spiritual masters.

"Seek rather not to contend. We know that where there is no contention, there is neither defeat nor victory. The supple willow does not contend against the storm, yet it survives."
—Master Po, *Kung Fu*

In another instance, Caine learns what is at the heart of philosophy and what, in fact, is at the heart of his own search for his missing brother. Fighting evil (which Caine does really, really well; David Carradine kicks serious evil butt in every episode of the show) isn't enough. There must be a positive striving behind each act.

Master Kan: Deal with evil through strength, but affirm the god in man through trust. In this way, we are prepared for evil, but we encourage good.

Kwai Chang Caine: And is good our great reward for trusting?

Master Kan: In striving for an ideal, we do not seek rewards. Yet trust does sometimes bring with it a great reward, even greater than good.

Kwai Chang Caine: What is greater than good?

Master Kan: Love.

The original series of Kung Fu ended with Caine finding not only his brother Danny but his nephew and two cousins. In 1993 a second series, *Kung Fu: The Legend Continues*, began, this time with Chris Potter playing Caine's son, Peter, a police detective who's also been trained in kung fu. In this series, Caine takes over the role of the ancient sage, imparting Eastern wisdom to his son.

Caine: When there is a right path and a wrong path, choosing neither or hiding behind a cloak of neutrality is the same thing as choosing the wrong path.

Peter: Why?

Caine: Because the right path will never be explored.

THE WISDOM OF THE EIGHTFOLD PATH

Kung Fu was, as someone has said, "TV's first mystical Eastern Western." But a lot of the wisdom that Caine's advisers gave to him—and that he passed on to Peter in *Kung Fu: The Legend Continues*—was phrased in a very general way, often as a kind of riddle that Caine was expected to meditate on so that he could better understand the nature of Man and the Universe and things.

Buddhist teachings have some of this elusive quality. We can get a better idea of the heart of the philosophy when we examine the eightfold path that's at the heart of Buddhist spirituality.

Wisdom

Right View: Translated as "right perspective," this is the intellectual understanding of the true nature of reality; where suffering comes from, and how to get rid of it through following the eightfold path. Though this basic knowledge is the first step on the path, it can lead to deeper wisdom later after the Buddhist masters the art of concentration.

Right Intention: Once you have the right view down, then discerning the differences between right and wrong intention becomes possible.

Ethical Conduct

Right Speech: Absolutely no lying. Even if the Buddha asks you if he looks fat in those pants.

Right Action: No killing, no stealing, and no illicit sex. Basically, no fun.

> **"And what is right action? Abstaining from taking life, from stealing, and from unchastity."**
> —Saccavibhanga Sutta

Right Livelihood: Sorry Tony Soprano, you can't be a ruthless criminal and also reach enlightenment, according to the Buddha. What you do for a living matters. The following occupations are off-limits for Buddha:

Weapons: Weapons manufacturing and trading.

Human Trafficking/Prostitution: Slave trading, prostitution, or the buying and selling of children or adults.

Meat: Breeding animals for slaughter or selling slaughtered animals.

Intoxicants: Manufacturing or selling intoxicating drinks or addictive drugs.

Poison: Producing or trading in any kind of toxic product designed to kill.

And, of course, investment banking. Alex Keaton would have a rough time being a Buddhist.

Right Effort: Not only are you expected to try to stop doing and thinking bad things, but you now must exert your effort to stop evil from arising in the world. Be a real do-gooder.

Concentration

Right Mindfulness: Also translated as "right memory," right mindfulness requires you to be aware of your thoughts and how stimuli affect your mind and body. Pay attention and keep the mind open, aware, and playful. In other words, meditation is not the same thing as taking an afternoon nap.

Right Concentration: You must concentrate on an object of attention until reaching full concentration and a state of meditative absorption (*jhana*). Traditionally, the practice of *samadhi*, or meditation, can be developed through mindfulness of breathing (*anapanasati*), through visual objects (*kasina*), and through repetition of phrases (*mantra*).

> **"I forgot my mantra."**
> —Jeff Goldblum in *Annie Hall*

EARL HICKEY, KARMA CHAMELEON

Earl Hickey, main character in *My Name Is Earl*, doesn't exhibit the typical attributes of a *bodhisattva*, i.e., one who has achieved true enlightenment. In fact, he's a lowlife. He's jobless. He's a drunk. And he is an admitted thief, describing himself as someone who would "steal anything that wasn't nailed down."

> **"If you snatch enough purses, you learn a few things about Mace."**
> —Earl Hickey

If this weren't bad enough, whatever misery Earl doesn't cause himself, it seems the universe causes for him. He's a truly unlucky guy. When he was born, he was supposed to be named "Carl" after his dad, but an extra loop in cursive made him Earl. After a night of heavy drinking, he married Joy (Jaime Pressly), six months pregnant at the time. Later, the loving couple had a son of their own—or so Earl thought. When the son was born black, Earl figured something must be wrong. He was right. Turns out the real father of the boy was Darnell, the owner of Earl's favorite drinking hole, Ernie's Crab Shack.

To everyone's amazement, Earl stays with his unfaithful wife and faithfully annoying illegitimate children. To Earl's amazement, his wife stays with him and his lazy brother, who sleeps on the couch all day.

Then, one day, Earl's bad luck changes dramatically when he wins $100,000 on a lottery ticket. Seconds later, while celebrating feverishly on the street, Earl is struck by a car. When he regains consciousness in the hospital, he realizes that his winning ticket is lost.

FROM CARSON DALY'S MOUTH TO BUDDHA'S EARS

Lying helpless and hopeless in the hospital bed, Earl looks up at the TV to hear Carson Daly, host of *Last Call with Carson Daly*, explain to his guest, Tracy Adkins, that the secret of his success is karma. "Do good deeds, and good things will happen to you," says Carson. Earl's mind is blown.

Earl makes a list of everything and everyone he has harmed in his life. We then follow him on a journey to right these wrongs, and heal these people. On his first mission of goodness, he decides to pick up trash. Karma answers Earl quickly, as he finds his missing winning lottery ticket in the trash.

> **"You know the kind of guy who does nothing but bad things, and then wonders why his life sucks? Well . . . that was me. Every time something good happened to me, something bad was always waiting around the corner. Karma. That's when I realized I had to change."**
> —Earl Hickey

You Are Karma's Bitch and Then You Die

Karma is the main recurring theme of *My Name Is Earl*, affecting all the characters—not just Earl but other characters as well. Earl will even address karma directly, as if he were talking to God. Karma's power and influence are clearly recognized and respected by Earl, who once proclaims, "I am karma's bitch." With karma on his side, Earl makes a serious effort to check off each of his items on his list and be a real do-gooder in the world. But is karma what is driving Earl to do good internally, or is it just the consequences of his good deeds? That's the question that the show keeps asking—and never quite answers.

Earl's motivation is obviously self-serving, which is what makes *My Name Is Earl* philosophically interesting. If Earl were genuinely interested in making up for his past actions from the start, there would be little to debate philosophically. Noble motivation + noble action = noble person. That's clear. But what about this equation: ignoble motivation + noble action = ? Some philosophers, such as Immanuel Kant, believe that it's the thought that counts, while others, like John Stuart Mill, say that only actions matter. Most of us fall somewhere in between.

That is not to say that Earl does not change during the course of the series. While the karma project starts out totally self-serving, there are moments in which Earl begins to sincerely wish to make up for his past, like the time when Earl confronts Maggie, a bearded woman whom he used to torment as a child. After spending some time with her he begins to appreciate her for who she is on the inside. Minutes later he is about to make fun of some circus freaks when he catches himself: "What good is it to cross Maggie off my list if I'm gonna keep doing the same thing to other people?" Indeed, Earl. Indeed.

CHAPTER 19

Lost But Not Least

Lost, one of modern TV's outstanding phenomena, started broadcasting on ABC in 2004 and ran until 2010. The show had some of the highest ratings for recent dramas, even amid occasional criticism that it seemed at times as if the writers were making things up as they went along. In the final season, each episode averaged 11 million viewers, and the end of the show is still a subject of controversy among fans.

The show followed the fortunes of the survivors of a plane crash on an uncharted island. The island, it turned out, is haunted by other entities, called, not surprisingly, "the Others." As the show went on, a number of the original characters were killed off and, in some cases, replaced by other characters. The show involved, among other things, supernaturalism, time travel, and the conflict between science and faith.

In this chapter, we'll revisit some of the themes introduced in Chapter 10, in which we looked at the conflicting visions of human society held by John Locke and Thomas Hobbes. *Lost* brings those visions into sharp relief.

LOST, FOUND, AND LOST AGAIN

It is no coincidence that in the TV show *Lost* the characters John Locke and Jack Shephard are named after two philosophers—John Locke and Jean-Jacques Rousseau—both of whom theorized about how man would fare without all the complex burdens and restraints of modern society, in a pure "state of nature."

In Locke's state of nature, we are all born free—masters of our own domain. We are all born equal with the same natural rights—rights that are derived solely from our nature as rational agents, not from any king or government. Among these rights are life, liberty, and property (in the Declaration of Independence, Jefferson preferred the phrase "pursuit of happiness" to the less evocative "property").

Without some external authority, individuals, while free, are vulnerable—our inherent rights in jeopardy. To protect these natural rights, individuals band together to form governments. The right of these governments to rule derives solely from the consent of the governed. Legitimate governments then are governments that are formed by the people and for the people, while illegitimate governments derive their power from coercion and conquest or divine right, a concept Locke and his contemporary liberals rejected. The radical implication is that if a government infringes upon the natural rights of its citizens, it can and should be overthrown.

Locke: We were all brought here for a reason.

Jack: Who brought us here John?

Locke: The Island.

Locke and the Individual

John Locke the character is not so-named because he expresses Lockean views or carries around a copy of a Viking Portable collection of the works of the British philosopher. Rather he embodies a spirit of uncompromising individualism. Locke doesn't like to be told what to do—or what he is capable of. "Don't tell me what I can do!" is Locke's catch phrase when someone tries to limit his freedom. Locke goes his own way from the beginning despite Jack Shephard's rapid ascension to group leader. Locke is willing to go so far as to use physical violence against other survivors if he feels it's right—at one point he ties up Boone to prevent him from telling Jack and the other survivors about the mysterious hatch, which the characters find in season one.

Locke, unlike the other survivors, has a reason to embrace the mysterious danger of the island: He has come out of the plane crash with a miraculous ability to use his previously useless legs. With a new and profound embrace of life, Locke would rather go it alone than follow orders—a proud lone wolf roaming free in the state of nature.

Being Lost Ain't That Bad-Unless You're with Hobbes

Jean-Jacques Rousseau shares Locke's generally romantic conception of man in the state of nature. This stands in stark contrast to Hobbes, a philosopher whose vision of a world without government is a dark one in which "every man is at war with every other man." It isn't that Hobbes thinks we are all born evil; it's just that without a government enforcing law, man will find it impossible to cooperate in any meaningful way for fear of being screwed by the other.

Think of a standoff between two gunmen. Each may want to put the gun down, but each is too afraid that the other will not. To use a broader analogy, individuals regard each other in the Hobbesian state of nature the way the United States and the USSR regarded each other during the Cold War—that is, with deep suspicion. Thus Hobbes's belief that the best form of government is a strong one, like a monarchy, that has the power, in a sense, to keep the peace amongst men.

ROUSSEAU AND REVOLUTION

The philosopher Rousseau's state of nature, like Locke's, is Club Med by comparison. Rousseau romanticized the notion of the "noble savage," a fiercely independent individual living outside the repressive and oppressive structure of modern society.

Jean-Jacques Rousseau (1712–1778) lived in Geneva, Switzerland, where he was comparatively free to develop his heretical social doctrines. He tells us that he steeped himself in Classical literature (like Augustine, he wrote an autobiography that he, too, titled *Confessions*), while forming a liaison with an older woman. She supported him financially and he eventually moved to Paris, where he plunged into the intellectual life of the French capital. He managed to make friends with all the leading intellectuals of his day and quarreled with almost all of them at one time or another. After some years, he returned to Geneva, where he lived for much of the rest of his life.

His most important philosophic works include *Emile* (which is about his theories of education) and *The Social Contract*.

One of the ideas that Rousseau put forward was that of the "noble savage." The idea is that human nature is distorted and perverted by civilization. "Man is born free," Rousseau declares in ringing tones at the beginning of *The Social Contract*, "but everywhere is in chains." If man is born out of society, free from its restrictions, he will find true freedom. Nonetheless, Rousseau understands that some measure of civilization is necessary, so he sees a constant tension between man's natural freedom and those freedoms that are granted him by governments.

The Other Rousseau

Back on *Lost*, Danielle Rousseau, who has managed to survive on the island for sixteen years completely alone, represents Rousseau's idea of the noble savage. That said, even the most noble savage needs the companionship of other noble savages—we are social animals, after all. Rousseau the character is shell-shocked from too much time alone in the state of nature. And she has reasons to be scared—the state of nature can be a deadly and anarchic place.

The character Mikhail Bakunin, a member of the Others who shares his name with a famous Russian anarchist, embodies the darker side of the state of nature. He expresses this anarchy when he shoots Ms. Klugh, an authority figure of his people, the Others. Bakunin would completely understand Rousseau's idea that although the state of nature is our original and pure condition, it's full of dangers.

While Locke (the philosopher, not the character) focused on our ability to reason, Rousseau wrote a lot about the human capacity for empathy, or as he calls it, "pity." There is a natural human instinct to abhor watching another human being suffer. This "pity," according to Rousseau, serves to "mitigate . . . the ferocity of his egocentrism."

> **"Although modesty is natural to man, it is not natural to children. Modesty only begins with the knowledge of evil."**
> —Jean-Jacques Rousseau

The creators of *Lost* share Rousseau's vision of human nature and what life looks like outside the civilized society. Sure the island is a dangerous place, but these strangers show compassion or pity for one another from the start. In fact, the show begins with Dr. Jack Shephard going back into the plane wreckage to help save strangers, putting his own life in danger. Throughout the series, almost all of our favorite castaways surprise us with a moment of heroism, a moment when they put others ahead of themselves. Jack and Kate make a habit of it.

Rousseau (again, the philosopher, not the character) would argue that the most important way in which we can transform the dichotomy between natural freedom and civilization is through education—which is why he wrote so much about it.

> **"We are born weak, we need strength; helpless, we need aid; foolish, we need reason. All that we lack at birth, all that we need when we come to man's estate, is the gift of education."**
> —Jean-Jacques Rousseau

ANOTHER STORY WITHOUT THE OTHERS?

Some thinkers have made the argument that a common enemy forces people to band together. Think of the wave of patriotism that swept this nation after Pearl Harbor or 9/11. It is clear that preparing for war with another nation can serve to bring this nation together. If this is true for a huge country like the United States, how much more is it true for a small group of plane crash survivors stranded on an island populated with smoke monsters, weird whispers, and, of course, the Others?

What if the survivors did not have the Others to worry about? Would the group splinter as in *The Lord of the Flies?* And would those kids in *The Lord of the Flies* have gone bananas if they had been able to channel their fear and hate into the destruction of a common enemy?

Carl Schmitt asserted an even more drastic view, that a common enemy is not only useful in creating social cohesion and cooperation, but actually necessary. War is a necessity. Of course, Schmitt was a Nazi, but maybe in this instance he's on to something.

LOST IN TIME

Time travel has been a popular plot device for centuries, but hardly something anyone took seriously. Einstein changed all that. Instead of a universe in which space and time were separate phenomena, Einstein's wacky universe is bound together in a single fabric of space-time. One of the profound implications of Einstein's theory of relativity was that if an object were to travel fast enough—near the speed of light—it could change its passage through time. Suddenly, traveling through time became less science fiction, and more scientific possibility.

But Einstein's theories just show that it's possible to travel into the future, not the past. For instance, according to relativity, if you took a trip in a space ship away from Earth near the speed of light (the cosmic speed limit) and then back, a few years could have passed in the ship while thousands of years could pass on Earth. This is because there is no "objective" time, no universal clock. There is just subjective time. Your subjective time was a couple of years, the Earth's was thousands of years.

Going into the past would require traveling faster than the speed of light (the fastest thing in the universe, according to Einstein) or the use of wormholes to zip through the space-time continuum. And—the more interesting question explored in *Lost*—if you could travel back in time, could you change the past? Could you change what has already happened? For instance, how can you go back in time and kill your grandmother before she gave birth to your mother, since doing so would preclude your existing? Remember those paradoxes of Zeno that we talked about at the beginning of the book? They're starting to look easy now, aren't they?

Russian physicist Igor Novikov argued that while time travel was possible (according to the theories of relativity and quantum mechanics), it would only be possible to interact with the past, not alter it. Enter Desmond David Hume.

THE QUANTUM LEAPING TIME TUNNEL

Television took up time travel before *Lost*, notably in *Quantum Leap* (NBC, 1989–1993) and *The Time Tunnel* (ABC, 1966–1967). Both these shows got around Einstein's theory by pretending it didn't exist. In *Quantum Leap*, Dr. Sam Beckett, played by Scott Bakula, could leap into any period between his present and the date of his birth. This weird restriction meant that he was spared the perils of time travelers James Darren and Robert Colbert on *The Time Tunnel*, who were always being transported into dangerous situations.

Their first trip landed them on board the *Titanic* on her 1912 maiden voyage. On subsequent trips, they visited Pearl Harbor and Devil's Island, in time to meet political prisoner Alfred Dreyfus (falsely accused of treason, in one of the major political scandals of late nineteenth-century France).

TIME TRAVEL RULES: GET LOST!

Scottish philosopher David Hume (1711–1776) wrote extensively on the relationship between free will and determinism. Do we have the freedom to choose or don't we? Hume thought that while we did "choose" one thing over another, we are in actuality following the dictates of our passions.

Fellow Scotsman Desmond Dave Hume of *Lost* has a special burden. He is the only person who can change time in the normal world, the world outside the Island. These are the two exceptions to the rules of time travel in the Lost universe: the Island (everyone can change time on the Island, which is why all of our favorite Losties have to go back) and Desmond. The "rules don't apply to you," the scientist Daniel Faraday tells Desmond as he tries to convince a confused Desmond that he is the key to saving the lives of the Losties years into the future. But can Desmond fundamentally change what has already happened?

Eloise Hawking (who shares a last name with physicist genius Stephen Hawking) warns him he will not be able to do this, that time can't be changed. At first, it seems that she's right, and his efforts seem futile. Hume can only defer another character's death, not stop it entirely. The universe, it seems, will correct itself. Philosopher David

Hume's deterministic theory is reflected by Desmond's uphill struggle against fate.

A Black Swan. LOL. Get Lost, Already!

For centuries, everyone assumed that swans were white because there had never been a case where a swan wasn't white. Then someone found black swans in Australia. Well, there went the theory that all swans are white. It only takes one to prove that this is not the case.

No matter how many times you witness something in the past, this is still not proof that it will be that way in the future. Hume called this the "black swan" metaphor. Strictly speaking, according to this way of thinking, there's no absolute proof that we're going to die at some point. Just because everyone else who's ever lived has died, that's not proof that we will. Maybe we're different.

When it comes to traveling through time and altering the past to change the future, is Desmond David Hume a black swan?

BACKWARD, FORWARD, AND SIDEWAYS

Starting in season five, there are three timelines in *Lost*: that of Jack and those who left the Island; that of Sawyer and the other survivors stuck on the Island, skipping around through time until eventually ending up in 1973; and the sideways timeline of a parallel universe taking place on the mainland in which our favorite Losties were never lost at all, since Flight 815 never crashed.

LOSING YOUR RELIGION . . . OR YOUR FAITH IN SCIENCE

The tension between faith and reason, between the man of science and the man of faith, is explored in *Lost* through the struggle between John Locke and Dr. Jack Shephard. At first, they are both men of science, both empiricists of the first order. That is to say, they rely on the evidence of their eyes, what can be physically proven. But Locke quickly moves to spiritualism as he comes to see the Island as a special place. As early as the second episode, Locke tells Shephard he is seeing someone who in reality cannot be there.

> "I'm a meat and potatoes kind of guy, Jack . . . I'm not a believer in magic. But this place is different. It's special . . . Was your White Rabbit a hallucination? Probably. But what if everything that happened here is for a reason? What if the person you are seeing is really there?"
>
> —John Locke, *Lost*

Increasingly convinced of the magical nature of the island, Locke begins to transform from a "meat and potatoes" skeptic to the resident Island guru, a man of faith rather than a man of science. Slowly, his Eastern consciousness beings to emerge. He becomes convinced that everyone is on that island "for a reason." There are no more coincidences for the newly Taoist Locke.

Jack, the doctor, the scientist, remains traditionally Western in his skepticism. He refuses to believe in a world—or an Island—where each man is not in total control of his destiny, where we do not have complete freedom to make choices as well as the responsibility that results from wielding such freedom. As Locke and Jack struggle to lead the group in the "right" direction, the conflict between Jack's skepticism and Locke's spiritualism reaches a breaking point when Jack, holding a gun, refuses to press the button in the hatch that is supposed to be pressed every 108 minutes according to a video left by the Dharma Initiative. Jack will not be a slave to forces that are not under his control.

Locke: [trying to convince Jack to push the button in the hatch] You saw the film, Jack. This is a . . . this is a two person job, at least.

Sayid Jarrah: This argument is irrelevant. [goes to push the button]

Jack: Sayid, don't.

Sayid: Jack.

Jack: Don't. It's not real. Look, you want to push the button, you do it yourself.

Locke: If it's not real, then what are you doing here, Jack? Why did you come back? Why do you find it so hard to believe?

Jack: Why do you find it so easy?

Locke: It's never been easy!

Kate Austen: Maybe you should just do it.

Jack: No . . . [less convinced]

Jack: It's a button.

Locke: [pleading] I can't do this alone, Jack . . . I don't want to.

[echoing the word of his former girlfriend]

Locke: It's a leap of faith, Jack.

Jack, realizing that perhaps not pushing the button is as dangerous an act of faith as pushing it, decides to give in and push the button. At that moment, the stubbornly skeptical and fiercely independent scientist Dr. Jack Shephard becomes the thing he fears most of all—a slave to some imaginary force—a slave to something unknown, unheard, and unmasked.

Just Plain Lost

Finally, characters are "lost" in their own personal lives, lost in the sense that they do not know who they are. Sawyer is a con man without an ounce of social grace or empathy for others in the beginning of the series, but by the end of it he has shown himself to be a leader, a man capable of acts of true heroism. There is Kate, the fugitive who is literally running from the law. There is Sayid, a man lost between the worlds of his gentle loving nature and the cruel acts of torture he has committed in his past. And then there is Jack and Locke and Hugo Hurley Reyes, all of whom have some serious daddy issues.

On the Island, all of the characters (with the exception of Michael Dawson), become far better people. They crash on that Island a group of guarded strangers afraid of their own shadow—and their own past. The Island, in the end, brings out their best selves.

Conclusion

"How can you put on a meaningful drama when, every fifteen minutes, proceedings are interrupted by twelve dancing rabbits with toilet paper?"
—Rod Serling

"Television! Teacher, mother, secret lover."
—Homer Simpson

Some people think that philosophy is what's taught in stuffy classrooms by professors who smell like mothballs and who are hauling out the same hoary texts they've been using for thirty years to drone on and on about a bunch of dead white guys. So who really cares?

As we hope you realize after reading this book, you should care. Because philosophy, whether from a book or from a TV show, is about the great problems in life. It's not just these strange, abstract questions like, "What do we really know?" and "What is the nature of being?" Philosophy is also about very practical questions:

- How can we live together?
- Is it ever right to injure someone else?
- Is my life predetermined by forces beyond my control?
- What happens after I die?

And much, much more.

Does television help us answer these questions? Of course. Because TV is also about life. Sometimes, as in the case of *Three's Company* or *Sarah Palin's Alaska*, it may seem pretty far removed from life as we know it, but if it weren't familiar to us on some level, we wouldn't watch it. And philosophy is all about life. About those important life questions that TV shows take up constantly.

Does TV have the answers? Not all of them, certainly. But if you watch enough and keep an open mind, you can at least figure out what some of the questions are. And that's an important start to looking at the world in a whole different way.

Meanwhile, remember that those dead white guys back in ancient Greece may not have been able to answer all the questions on *Jeopardy* or win the money on *Who Wants to Be a Millionaire*, but that doesn't mean they weren't smart. After all, two and a half thousand years later, we're still asking the same questions they were. It's just that the answers seem to have gotten a bit more complicated.

Earlier, when we were talking about St. Augustine and Thomas Aquinas, we got into the subject of Free Will. This is one of the most complicated questions that philosophy has to deal with: If there's a

God, does he or she allow us to do what we want, even if it hurts other people? And if there's no god, what stops us from doing whatever we want to one another?

Sometimes, a person doesn't do something because she or he doesn't want to. And sometimes, that's the best reason of all.

The Howdy Doody Show ran from 1947 to 1960—one of the longer-running children shows in the history of television. Beside the nauseatingly adorable freckle-faced marionette that was the "star" of the show, it included a number of long-running characters such as the human host Buffalo Bob Smith, marionettes Heidi Doody (Howdy's sister), Mayor Phineas T. Bluster, Sandra the Witch, and Captain Windy Scuttlebutt, and Clarabell the Clown.

Clarabell was human and was played, for some years, by Bob Keeshan, who went on to be Captain Kangaroo. After he left the show, Clarabell was played by the jazz musician Lew Anderson.

On the very last episode of the show, broadcast on September 24, 1960, Buffalo Bob learned to his surprise that Clarabell, who'd remained silent all through the show's run, could actually speak.

"You can *talk*," Buffalo Bob said in amazement. "Well, Clarabell, this is your last chance! If you really can talk, prove it . . . let's hear you say something!"

Clarabell turned to face the cameras and, a tear in the corner of his eye, said, "Goodbye, kids."

Sometimes, philosophers will tell you, that's all that needs to be said.

APPENDIX A

Glossary of Philosophical Terms

Not all these terms and philosophers appear in this book, but you'll find them a useful starting point for further investigation. Toss some of these around at parties if you want to sound really smart.

Absolute, The—Hegel's name for the ultimate reality.

Aesthetics—The school of philosophy that ponders the nature of art and beauty. Schopenhauer recommended it as one of the ways to keep earthly passions at bay.

Alienation—The feeling of isolation, of not being part of society. Expressed by Hegel, Kierkegaard, and the Existentialists.

Altruism—Looking out for the next fellow and trying to do good works. Some philosophers believe altruism is impossible, because all actions, even charitable ones, are motivated by self-interest. The Objectivists think it is a downright foolish practice.

Angst—Deep anxiety, which many philosophers, including Hegel, Kierkegaard, Sartre, and Camus, believe is an unavoidable emotional state for any thinking man or woman.

Anthropomorphism—Assigning human qualities and characteristics to nonhuman things, including nature and God.

Ápeiron—The Greek word for "boundless." This was Anaximander's way to describe the boundless reality, as opposed to the other Monists, who made one of the elements the basis for all reality.

Aphorism—Nietzsche's main technique for philosophizing. A pithy observation that can vary in length from a few lines to a few paragraphs.

A posteriori—Latin for "after." A statement, concept, or idea that is determined after the fact, based on experience or observation.

A priori—Latin for "before." A statement, concept, or idea that is a given and does not need to be based on experience or observation.

Atomism—The belief of pre-Socratic philosophers that everything could be broken down into tiny, indivisible particles called atoms. Pretty insightful, because it turned out to be true (until scientists learned that the atom could be split into subatomic particles).

Behaviorism—The psychological school of thought that espoused that the best way to study humans is by observing their behavior, not delving into the depths of the unconscious. B. F. Skinner is the most well-known psychological behaviorist.

Calculus of Felicity—Jeremy Bentham's strange mathematical formula wherein we can calculate the pain/pleasure factor of an act before indulging in it.

Cogito ergo sum—Descartes's famous "I think, therefore I am" proves that you can be certain of at least one reality in this crazy world: You exist because you are thinking thoughts right now.

Consequentialism—Another name for the Utilitarian philosophy. The consequences of an action determine its value. From a Utilitarian perspective, this philosophy means seeking pleasure and avoiding pain.

Dasein—Martin Heidegger's word for what he called "Being There," a fully realized conscious approach to life, more than merely "stayin' alive."

Deconstructionism—The process of breaking down a thing (in Jacques Derrida's case, language) to show that what is being stated is in fact inherently false.

Deism—The religious faith that likens God to a cosmic watchmaker. The universe is an orderly, perfectly functioning, yet impersonal cosmos. God designed it and now it more or less runs itself.

Dialectic—The Socratic Dialogue, a series of questions and answers to help the person discover the truth for themselves, rather than simply telling them. The term is also applied to Hegel's triad of Thesis-Antithesis-Synthesis.

Dualism—The view that each person is two entities, a mind with mental attributes and a body with physical attributes, instead of a single entity with attributes of both sorts.

Empiricism—The philosophy that maintains that all knowledge is gathered through sensory experience alone. The opposite of Rationalism.

Enlightenment—Also called the Age of Reason. During the eighteenth century, the age of Voltaire and the other philosophers.

Epistemology—Another word for the theory of knowledge.

Eternal recurrence—Nietzsche's proposition that we live the same life, without variation, over and over again. He probably did not mean this literally. He was suggesting that we should make our lives such that we would not mind repeating it time and again.

Existentialism—The philosophy that expresses the belief that life is meaningless and absurd, and the best that we can do is try to lead authentic, heroic lives in a cold and uncaring world.

Forms—Plato's doctrine that Ideas exist independently, beyond their physical and mental counterparts. For example, there is a Form of

"Beauty" out there in the ether, and things of beauty we see in physical reality are mere shadows of the Form.

Functionalism—Emile Durkheim's theory that a society, in essence, takes on a personality of its own and can be objectively viewed the way a scientist or physician may regard a living organism.

Hedonism—The belief that the pursuit of pleasure and the avoidance of pain is the greatest goal of mankind. Social Hedonism was at the foundation of the Utilitarian philosophy.

Idealism—The belief that everything is "in the mind," and physical reality does not exist. Made famous by George Berkeley.

Illumination—Divinely inspired insight and wisdom. St. Augustine believed that this was a necessary ingredient to true knowledge.

Immanent—Something that is directly experienced. The opposite of transcendent.

Innate ideas—Thoughts are observations that can come without benefit of sensory experience. This was the belief of the Rationalists, and the opposite viewpoint of the Empiricists.

Logical atomism—Bertrand Russell and Ludwig Wittgenstein's theory that language and concepts could, like physical elements, be broken down into their smallest particulars and thereby logically analyzed.

Materialism—The belief that reality is composed of physical matter. The opposite of Idealism.

Monism—The belief that one element or thing is the basic stuff of reality. The pre-Socratic philosophers were Monists.

Natural selection—Charles Darwin's theory of evolution. Members of a species that are best adapted for reproduction flourish, altering the species over time as those unable to adapt die off.

Nihilism—The ultimate in a despairing, negative worldview. Utter hopelessness.

Nominalism—The medieval belief that opposed the Aristotelian theory of Universals.

Noumena—Kant's name for the metaphysical world, the reality that lies beyond our ability to perceive.

Objectivism—Ayn Rand's popular twentieth-century view that combines rugged individualism and laissez-faire capitalism.

Ockham's Razor—The philosophical version of the slogan "Keep it simple." The simplest solution to a problem or question is also usually the correct one.

Othering—Michel Foucault's name for the way people distinguish themselves from other people, usually in a pejorative way.

Pantheism—The belief that God is Nature, not an all-powerful entity in Heaven but a force that surrounds and permeates the world.

Paradox—A seemingly contradictory concept. It consists of several propositions, each true in itself, that cannot collectively be true.

Phenomenology—The study of consciousness in and of itself, leaving the empirical world out of the equation altogether.

Philosophes—The name for the French philosophers of the Enlightenment. It is the French word for "philosophers."

Philosophy—Literally the "love of wisdom," from the Greek words *philia* and *sophia*.

Polis—The Greek word for city-state. Athens was a city-state. The word *politics* comes from *polis*.

Postmodernism—The current state of philosophy falls under the label of Postmodernism. Perhaps future generations will have another name for this era.

Predestination—The belief that your fate is determined before you are born, and nothing you do in this life will make a difference whether you go to Heaven or Hell.

Pre-Socratic philosophers—The group of philosophers who came before Socrates. They are also called Monists because they offered theories that the nature of reality was composed of one thing (water, air, fire, numbers, and so on).

Rationalism—The philosophy of Descartes, Spinoza, and Leibniz. They believed that there are innate ideas in the mind and not everything we know must necessarily be gathered through sensory experience.

Relativism—The belief that things such as morality vary from society to society and culture to culture, and none is better or worse than any other.

Social contract—A relationship between the citizens and the people. It could be formally agreed upon or an unwritten, implicit agreement. Thomas Hobbes, John Locke, and Jean-Jacques Rousseau all had versions of what they felt was the ideal social contract.

Sophistry—The frivolous misuse of philosophy to teach how to win arguments and sway opinions via linguistic legerdemain.

Syllogism—Aristotle's logical argument, which has two premises and a conclusion. The famous example is, "All men are mortal. Socrates is a man. Therefore, Socrates is mortal."

Tabula rasa—Latin for "blank slate." Many philosophers, including John Locke and Voltaire, believed that we are born with an empty mind, ready to have sensory experiences imprinted on our brains.

Things-in-themselves—This is Kant's name for the Noumenal world, the metaphysical reality beyond the limited reality that we can perceive, which he called the *phenomenal world*.

Transcendent—Something beyond the realm of ordinary experience. The opposite of immanent.

Universals—Aristotle's spin on Platonic Forms. He believed that the Forms were within the physical object, not separate entities in another dimension.

Utilitarianism—The philosophy of Jeremy Bentham and John Stuart Mill, which suggests that the ultimate goal of individuals and society should be the maximization of pleasure and the minimization of pain.

APPENDIX B
Who's Who in Philosophy

Although not all these figures are discussed in this book, this list will serve as a guide for you if you'd like to do some more reading on the subject.

Thales—Thales of Miletus is often designated as the first "official" philosopher. He is regarded as the founder of natural philosophy. He proposed that everything is composed of water. Though Thales could not have known that the human body is composed of mostly water, he was on to something, simplistic as his theories may seem today. His rational approach of not attributing anything and everything to "the gods" paved the way for the scientific method. He was revered as a sage in his lifetime and long after his death.

Anaximander—A younger contemporary of Thales, he didn't believe that it was one of the four familiar elements that was the basic stuff of the world; rather, all those elements and more all comprised a common element he, for lack of a better word, called "The Boundless." All things arise from The Boundless (*ápeiron* in Greek), and all things return to The Boundless. This foreshadows Einstein's dictum that "Matter can neither be created nor destroyed."

Anaximenes—A pupil of Anaximander who digressed from his mentor's theory by singling out air as the root of all things. We need air as much as water. He believed the soul was composed of air.

Heraclitus—Nicknamed "the Obscure," Heraclitus was a philosopher who was known as something of a downer. His theory that everything is composed of fire, if taken metaphorically, is expressed in his belief that everything is in flux. You couldn't even step into the same river twice, according to him, because the flowing water was not the same water you dipped your big toe into mere seconds before.

Parmenides—The anti-Heraclitus; he wrote in direct response to him. Simply put, he believed that there is no flux; in fact, everything is stagnant. "It is" was his credo. Being is immutable and constant, and change is an illusion.

Zeno of Elea—Zeno is best known for a couple of famous paradoxes. The first one explains how, sitting in your room, you can never really reach the door. If the distance between two points is composed of an infinite number of points, then we can bisect that line. And we can keep bisecting the areas we previously bisected ad infinitum. Hence, you potentially have an infinite amount of space in a finite distance between two points and can never really get anywhere.

The second of Zeno's paradoxes deals with motion. When you move from one place to another, you reach the midway point before the final destination. And before you get to the halfway mark, you reach the halfway mark of the midway point. Ergo, you have to travel an infinite number of points in a finite amount of time. And that is impossible, right?

Empedocles—Empedocles can be compared to Pythagoras in that he combined the scientific and spiritual, yet his area of expertise was medicine rather than mathematics. He also offered the theory that it was not one element at the center of it all, but rather that the roots of all four elements—fire, air, earth, and water—could be found in everything. The four roots would exist in different degrees. Obviously, water would have a preponderance of water roots, but the others would be there to a lesser degree. And in an ancient Greek variation on the yin/yang belief of coexisting complementary opposites, he added that the entities he called Love and Strife were complementary forces that impacted on the world as they knew it.

Anaxagoras—He took the theories of four roots a step further by declaring that reality can be reduced to an infinite number of "seeds." Not unlike Empedocles' hypothesis, these seeds contain elements of everything and are in everything, yet certain elements are there in greater abundance, creating life's myriad diversity. And in lieu of Empedocles' Love and Strife theory, Anaxagoras postulated on the existence of a *Nous*, or omniscient yet impersonal Mind, that gave order and constancy to the universe.

Leucippus and **Democritus**—The first to theorize that the world was composed of tiny particles called atoms. These particles were invisible to the human eye yet ubiquitous in their myriad combinations, comprising what we commonly call reality. Democritus built on the theories of Leucippus by suggesting that atoms were indivisible.

Protagoras—The first Sophist, he had a successful career and enjoyed great fame in his lifetime. "Man is the measure of all things" was his credo. This was not to suggest the nobility and evolutionary superiority of the species. It is actually an extreme case of relativism, moral and otherwise. "Anything goes" was the natural devolution of such a principle. If it feels good, do it. If it gets you ahead even at the expense of another, go for it.

Gorgias—He didn't put much stock in the notion of virtue, but instead felt that the power of persuasion was key. His philosophy is summed up in this three-pronged theory: Nothing exists; if anything did exist we could not know about it; and if something existed and someone knew about it, he or she couldn't communicate that awareness to others.

Prodicus—A rhetorician who, according to most accounts, was unabashedly in it for the money. Plato frequently satirized him as a pedantic lecturer on the niceties of language above all else. Eloquent and popular as he was, the officials of Athens saw fit to execute him for corrupting the young.

Socrates—This dynamic and controversial Athenian figure spent a lifetime in the public square engaging in dialogues with the young men of Athens. His singular method of posing questions to his intellectual quarry and drawing responses is called *Socratic Dialogue*. This form of question and answer and the logical debate of opposing views is called *dialectic*. Socrates' motto should be every philosopher's raison d'être: "The unexamined life is not worth living. Doing what is right is the only path to goodness, and introspection and self-awareness are the ways to learn what is right."

Plato—Plato was Socrates' most famous protégé. He continued the Socratic legacy while building on it with his own theories. Plato was a firm believer in Ideas, or as they are also called, Forms.

Aristotle—Aristotle studied under Plato as a student at the latter's Academy for twenty years. He was a prodigy and generally regarded as Plato's heir apparent. However, he disagreed with the master on several key points. Aristotle is famous for the syllogism, which is a logical argument that takes two truths, connects them, and arrives at a third truth.

Epicurus—One of the most misinterpreted philosophers in the pantheon of great thinkers in that his name and his philosophy became synonymous with wanton hedonism. Although Epicurus put great stock in the pursuit of pleasure, his definition of pleasure would be more akin to the delights enjoyed by the couch potato as opposed to the libertine. Epicurus led a restful, contemplative life, eating modestly, drinking moderately, and philosophizing for the most part from a prone position on his hammock.

Zeno of Citium—Founder of the Stoic school, he used to lecture from a temple porch, which was called a *stoa*, hence the name *Stoic*. The word *stoic* has remained in the language and defines a person who accepts life's slings and arrows without whining about it.

Marcus Aurelius—He was a foremost Stoic, whose collection of journal entries, *Meditations*, written in between vanquishing barbarian hordes, is a quintessential distillation of Stoic thought and practice.

Seneca—The Roman playwright and noted Stoic took his own life when he fell out of favor with the notorious emperor Nero.

Pyrrho of Elis—The founder of the Skeptic school of philosophy, he saw the road to happiness as doing as little as possible. Repose was the only recourse for the truly wise man. The only path to peace was to suspend judgment, because no worldview is any better than another. Do not believe anything you see or hear. Do not have any opinions. There is no such thing as good or evil. Rather than promote chaos and confusion, Pyrrho believed that to accept this is the only way to live.

Cicero—The famous Roman senator, lawyer, orator, and philosopher lived and died during some of the most turbulent times in ancient history. Cicero "Romanized" the Greek philosophers in Latin translations designed to bring the classics to the Romans. It is said he was inventive in his translations, and as a lifelong lawyer and politician, he had ulterior motives in his efforts to bring philosophy to the Roman Empire. Ever the pragmatist, he intended to use philosophy as a tool to further his political goals and advance the glory that was Rome. Though he was largely linked to the Roman branch of Skepticism, he was also a premier practitioner of Eclecticism.

Plotinus of Alexandria—The founder of Neoplatonist thought, he established a school in Rome. Neoplatonism was the last shout of ancient Greek philosophizing.

Augustine of Hippo—He was born and died in the last days of the Roman Empire and serves as a bridge between the classical and the medieval worlds. Augustine's candid autobiography, *Confessions*, chronicles his struggles with faith and earthly pleasures and contains the famous and ironic prayer, "God grant me chastity . . . but not yet." Augustine used Neoplatonic philosophy to defend, endorse, and affirm Christian theology. Augustine attempted to explain some of the many mysteries of Christianity through the philosophies of Plato.

Anselm of Canterbury—A Benedictine monk and teacher who ultimately became the Archbishop of Canterbury, the highest religious office in England. He sought to distinguish between philosophy and theology. The famous maxim of Anselm was *Credo ut intelligam*, which means "I believe that I may understand." He is most famous for his Ontological Argument, which "proves" the existence of God.

Thomas Aquinas—A prominent Catholic thinker who sought to Christianize Aristotle similarly to the way that Augustine adapted Neoplatonism to Christian teaching, he also reconciled the dilemma of Faith versus Reason. He is famous for his five points that prove the existence of God, and he spoke of Universals, his revised version of the Platonic Forms.

John Duns Scotus—Scotus was a Franciscan monk who endorsed many of the precepts of Augustine, yet differed on other key elements, including the necessity of "illumination." He believed humans have the intellect to comprehend God and his wonders without a celestial cheat sheet. Being a cleric and a man of his time, dogma rules as far as Scotus is concerned. He spins the notion of Universals by suggesting that they exist as Forms (to be found in the mind of God) and as part of the physical things they represent (as perceived in the mind of man). While Aquinas has the intellect pre-eminent over the human will, Scotus said that will is more important than intellect. This led to a great medieval debate known as the Thomist-Scotist controversy.

Roger Bacon—Bacon was a Franciscan monk who is regarded as a forerunner of the modern scientist. He sought to incorporate the academic disciplines of mathematics and language into theology and philosophy through his book *Opus Majus*. Bacon proposed that there are three ways to gain knowledge: authority, reason, and experience. He breaks experience into the realms of the internal and external. External experience is awareness of physical reality and the world of the senses. Internal experience is similar to Augustine's "illumination"—a little help from the person upstairs.

William of Ockham—Famous for the theory that has come to be known as Ockham's Razor, Ockham believed that when all is said and done in this crazy world, the simplest answer is usually the right one.

Francis Bacon—This British politician and businessman took a scientific approach to philosophy. He studied the world as an empirical observer would and attempted to avoid bringing his preconceptions and prejudices into the proceedings. Bacon proposed that, in order to truly understand the world, we must first be aware of the various obstacles and distractions that prevent us from seeing things clearly.

René Descartes—This French philosopher is often called the Father of Modern Philosophy. He started out his career as a mathematician and is credited with discovering the concept of analytic geometry. He uttered perhaps the most famous sentence in the history of philosophy: "I think, therefore I am." Everything could be questioned, but one thing remained a fact: the thinking of the thinker.

Thomas Hobbes—This English philosopher rejected Descartes's dualism and touted the theory that ours is a mechanistic and materialistic universe. An attempt to synthesize Empiricism and Rationalism, it is also quite a pessimistic viewpoint and paints man as a less than noble piece of work. His most famous work is called *The Leviathan*. The titular leviathan of Hobbes's tome is a society without order. Hobbes felt that without order, society would violently self-destruct.

Baruch Spinoza—Spinoza believed in *pantheism,* meaning that God is present in all things. Like Descartes, Spinoza wrestled with the idea of Substance. Descartes called the infinite substance God, while Spinoza called it Nature. His belief that God is Nature and that nature is one substance that can shape-shift into various forms that he called *modes* is not unlike the Monist philosophies of the pre-Socratics.

Gottfried Leibniz—While Spinoza spoke of modes, Leibniz believed that reality was made up of what he called *monads*. Like Democritus and the Atomists, Leibniz theorized that the smallest particle was called a *monad*. It was indivisible, as an atom was once believed to be, and each monad was as unique as a fingerprint. Everything, including people, is composed of monads, according to Leibniz.

John Locke—Locke was a British Empiricist who believed that all knowledge was gained through experience. There was no such thing as innate ideas, as he called them. He is famous for the theory of the *tabula rasa*, which means "blank slate" in Latin. Locke proposed that the human mind is a complete void upon birth and gradually accumulates data as it is exposed to life and its many sensory experiences.

George Berkeley—He believed that everything was an idea, even physical matter. Only minds and the ideas they generate are real, according to this Irish clergyman. He is considered to be the founder of the modern version of Idealism, a belief that goes back to Plato in its original presentation. Unlike the closet atheism of Locke, Berkeley flatly states that God is responsible for the introduction and dissemination of perceptions into the human brain. These things we perceive do not exist outside the mind. They have no substantial reality of their own.

David Hume—A Scottish philosopher who was influenced by and expanded upon the ideas of John Locke and George Berkeley, Hume not only denied the existence of the material substances of Locke, but also the spiritual world of ideas proposed by Berkeley. Hume also rejected the existence of the individual self. You do not exist. According to Hume, you are nothing more than what he called "a collection of different perceptions." He dismissed the scientific principle of cause-

and-effect and stated that knowledge of anything as certainty is just plain impossible, except maybe mathematics.

Montesquieu—Montesquieu was a noted jurist who spoke of relativism as it pertains to the law. Relativism is the belief that what is good for the goose may not necessarily be good for the gander. Montesquieu also proposed the notion of separation of powers in a government. He advocated a series of checks and balances in order to provide balance and thwart one element of government gaining more power than another.

Voltaire—One of the most famous and infamous philosophers of the Enlightenment, Voltaire was a celebrity and a controversial figure in his lifetime. His satirical pieces landed him in the Bastille, the notorious French prison, on more than one occasion, but these incarcerations did not cause his quill pen to run dry.

Jean-Jacques Rousseau—This French philosopher and social critic also was one of the earliest practitioners of the tell-all memoir. His candor was shocking in his day.

Mary Wollstonecraft—This was a woman truly ahead of her time. She wrote one of the most famous feminist rallying cries, *A Vindication of the Rights of Woman,* almost two hundred years before the modern feminist movement came into being. Her daughter, Mary Godwin, married the poet Percy Bysshe Shelley and wrote *Frankenstein.*

Ralph Waldo Emerson—Emerson was a writer and lecturer whose famous works include *Nature* and *Self-Reliance,* which expressed the

Transcendentalist philosophy. He viewed every individual as having full and free access to the Over-Soul. We are all something like cells in the giant organism that is God/Nature. We can access this collective unconsciousness and experience total interconnectedness with our fellows and the natural world. He believed that evil is not a force unto itself but merely arises from the absence of good. He considered poets to be the modern mystics and prophets and directly influenced and inspired America's greatest poet, Walt Whitman. His influence in philosophy and literature had a profound impact on American culture.

Henry David Thoreau—Famous for the book *Walden*, a journal of his solitary existence in a cabin on Walden Pond, Thoreau was an eloquent spokesperson for the Transcendentalist philosophy. Another philosophy that Thoreau espoused, and was later made better known and practiced in the twentieth century, was civil disobedience.

Auguste Comte—This French philosopher is generally regarded as the father of modern sociology. Comte sought to employ the same methods that scientists had used in the investigation and exploration of the physical world and apply them to the study of human affairs.

Karl Marx—He was the architect of what became modern socialism and communism, ideologies that went on to change the face of the globe and the state of the world in ways that Marx himself may never have imagined. A student of philosophy, he, along with Friedrich Engels, is the author of the world-altering work, *The Communist Manifesto*. He sought social reform to combat the injustices of the Industrial Revolution.

Max Weber—He was a German thinker who also took a jaundiced view of capitalism and sought to understand its emergence in the Western world rather than in another culture in another part of the world. He linked the rise of capitalism with the Protestant work ethic. Whereas Marx believed that economics motivated human thought, Weber believed the opposite: Human ideas brought about particular economic systems. And while Marx spoke of class struggles and ultimately class warfare, the word Weber used to describe the division of societies was *stratification*. Weber also addressed the rise of bureaucracies in Europe. He actually liked them! He thought they were the ideal organizing principle in the new industrial societies of Europe in the nineteenth century.

Émile Durkheim—He bridged the disciplines of sociology and the equally new notion of anthropology. Durkheim also founded the school of thought called *Functionalism*, which maintains that a society, in essence, took on a personality of its own and could be objectively viewed the way a scientist or physician may regard a living organism. He proposed that cultures have a *collective consciousness*, wherein the values and beliefs held by a culture direct the behavior of its members without them even knowing it.

Charles Darwin—The most famous proponent of the theory of evolution, he proposed the theory of natural selection in his book *On the Origin of Species*. This theory maintains that certain characteristics and qualities in a species enable it to survive, and thus those characteristics are passed on the progeny, over time altering the species in significant ways. Species went off in other directions while their progenitors remained stagnant or died away.

Herbert Spencer—This British philosopher put his spin on the evolutionary theory by applying it to humanity and calling it "survival of the fittest." This form of social Darwinism was often used to justify colonialism and the xenophobic European feelings of superiority.

Søren Kierkegaard—He was a literary figure in Denmark who used irony to make his points. As a result, it is often hard to tell when he is being serious and when he is pulling our collective philosophical leg. Kierkegaard is considered to be the first Existentialist. His views on alienation, the angst that plagues people, and the inherent absurdity of life influenced Jean-Paul Sartre, Albert Camus, and other twentieth-century Existentialists. They, however, were atheists while Kierkegaard remained a Christian throughout his life.

Friedrich Wilhelm Nietzsche—Perhaps the most controversial and most misunderstood philosopher, he was as much a literary figure as a philosopher. He had no formal philosophy and basically ranted in the form of aphorisms, short pithy quips, and pungent observations. Some of these include the notion that God is dead, the advocacy of the superman, the theory of eternal recurrence, and many more hot topics. His main targets were Western civilization and Christianity. A sensitive soul plagued by health problems, he ultimately descended into madness and never recovered.

Franz Boas—An influential anthropologist who sought to make anthropology more respectable, he believed in fieldwork, or living among the civilization you were studying for an extended period of time. He also rejected the ethnocentric and downright racist views of many of his predecessors. He trained a whole generation of anthropologists, and his work was the basis for the practice of cultural relativism.

Sigmund Freud—One of the most famous and influential psychologists of the twentieth century, his name is known by even those who don't know much about psychology. Two of the techniques of Freudian psychoanalysis are the interpretation of dreams and free association. Freud also came up with the infamous theory of the Oedipus Complex.

Carl Gustav Jung—The most famous follower of Sigmund Freud, Jung's most famous theory is that of the collective unconscious. This is a shared memory of symbols, imagery, and memories that he called *archetypes*, which hark back to the dawn of human consciousness and are common in all cultures and civilizations. Jung also proposed that within every man there is an inner woman and within every woman there is an inner man.

Alfred Adler—Another of Freud's students, Adler believed that feelings of inferiority rather than sexuality were the main motivating unconscious force in people.

William James—The father of American psychology and the brother of the novelist Henry James: His two-volume *Principles of Psychology* was the bible for a generation of American psychologists. His approach was called Functionalism. It proposed that the important purpose of psychological study was to examine the functions of consciousness. This involved longitudinal research, which is the process of studying selected subjects over lengthy periods of time by means of observation and tests.

B. F. Skinner—The most famous Behaviorist, he believed that people's behavior could be changed through the process of conditioning. The famous example of this involves the rat in a box (the box was designed by Skinner and is appropriately named the Skinner Box). The rat learned that if it presses a level, a food pellet is released. The positive reinforcement ensures that the behavior will be repeated; this is called *operant conditioning.*

Carl Rogers and **Abraham Maslow**—The pioneers of what was called *Humanistic Psychology*, they were dissatisfied with the rigidities of psychoanalysis and behaviorism. Their theories, neither psychoanalytic or behaviorist, came to be called the *third force.* These two men saw psychology as a means to help people fulfill their maximum potential. Rogers felt that all people are instilled with an innate drive to "be all that they can be," and it was the role of psychotherapy to facilitate this process. Abraham Maslow devised a hierarchy of needs, which is the path a person takes from the basic needs of survival on the road to the achievement of their potential. The lowest levels on the scale would be food and shelter, while further up the scale would be things like security and love. The top of the list of needs is what Maslow called *self-actualization.*

Jean Piaget—His main claim to fame is the work he did with children. After years working in schools and interviewing thousands of children, the Swiss psychologist identified four stages of childhood development. The sensorimotor stage, from birth to age two, involves the mastering of motor controls and learning to deal with the physical world. In the preoperational stage, from ages two to seven, the child focuses on verbal skills and communication. Kids begin to deal with numbers and other complex concepts in what Piaget called the concrete operational stage, and logic and reason evolves in the formal operational stage.

Edmund Husserl—The founder of phenomenology, this German philosopher endeavored to study the mind itself, not the outside world of things and events that the mind perceives. The proper study of consciousness is the mind, according to Husserl. He called this *phenomenological reduction.*

Martin Heidegger—His Existential philosophy influenced Camus, Sartre, and many modern philosophers that followed. Unlike Nietzsche, who posthumously suffered the slander of being labeled a Nazi, Heidegger has earned the title fair and square, publicly endorsing Hitler and the Nazis in the 1930s. He shifted the focus from the examination of conscious to experiencing the state of simply "being there" in his book *Being and Time.*

Bertrand Russell—A British philosopher, Nobel laureate, and one of the most influential philosophers of the twentieth century, Russell was also a pacifist. The fact that he also lived to the ripe old age of ninety-eight meant that he protested every major conflict from World War I to the Vietnam War. Although he did take a patriotic stand during World War II, in the Cold War he remained a staunch antinuclear weapons activist, writing a book expressing his concerns called *The Bomb and Civilization.* At the advanced age of eighty-nine, he was arrested at an antinuclear protest.

Ludwig Josef Johann Wittgenstein—This Austrian philosopher studied with Bertrand Russell and became an influential advocate of analytic and linguistic philosophy. In 1918, Wittgenstein completed the *Tractatus Logico-philosophicus*, which he called the "final solution" to all problems of philosophy. However, in later years, he began rejecting his own conclusions in the *Tractatus* and wrote yet another seminal work of modern philosophy called *Philosophical Investigations*.

Albert Camus—This French Algerian man of letters wrote *The Stranger*, *The Myth of Sisyphus*, and other novels, plays, and nonfiction works. He, along with Jean-Paul Sartre, was a premier exponent of Existentialism. Camus was given the Nobel Prize in Literature in 1957 and died tragically in a car accident in 1960. Although primarily known as a novelist and playwright, these were fictional devices that exposed existentialism to a wide audience.

Jean-Paul Sartre—The other French existentialist of the twentieth century was also a novelist and dramatist as well as the author of philosophical works and political polemics. He is more famous for the novel *Nausea*, the play *No Exit*, and the nonfiction work *Being and Nothingness*. He was also awarded the Nobel Prize for Literature, but unlike his fellow French existentialist Albert Camus, he turned it down.

Ayn Rand—An American novelist and philosopher, she is famous for the novels *The Fountainhead* and *Atlas Shrugged*. Her philosophy is called Objectivism. She put reason before emotion, and individualism over groupthink. She also thought egotism was a good thing, and altruism was a negative character trait.

Michel Foucault—This recent French philosopher is considered a postmodernist. Foucault's major works include *Madness and Civilization,* wherein he chronicled Western society's changing views toward mental illness over the centuries. Foucault's other major work is called *Discipline and Punish,* wherein he critiques the world's various penal systems making the case that—in the Western world at least—modern practices have made punishment into an industry controlled by professionals such as parole officers and psychologists.

Jacques Derrida—This contemporary French philosopher started the philosophical school called *deconstruction,* which is the process of breaking down something (in Derrida's case, language) to show that what is being stated is in fact inherently false.

Bibliography

BOOKS ABOUT PHILOSOPHY

Cathcart, Thomas, and Daniel Klein. *Plato and a Platypus Walk Into a Bar . . . : Understanding Philosophy Through Jokes*. New York: Penguin, 2007.

Durant, Will. *The Story of Philosophy*. New York: Pocket, 1991.

Jordan, James N. *Western Philosophy: From Antiquity to the Middle Ages*. New York: Macmillan, 1987.

Lavine, T. Z. *From Socrates to Sartre: The Philosophic Quest*. New York: Bantam, 1985.

Passmore, John. *A Hundred Years of Philosophy*. 2nd ed. New York: Penguin, 1966.

Randall, John Herman. *The Career of Philosophy*. Vol. I, *From the Middle Ages to the Enlightenment*. New York: Columbia University Press, 1962.

_____. *The Career of Philosophy*. Vol. II, *From the Enlightenment to the Age of Darwin*. New York: Columbia University Press, 1965.

Russell, Bertrand. *A History of Western Philosophy*. New York: Simon & Schuster, 1967.

Watson, Peter. *Ideas: A History of Thought and Invention, From Fire to Freud*. New York: Harper Perennial, 2006.

ORIGINAL SOURCES

Aristotle. *The Basic Works of Aristotle*. Edited by Richard McKeon. New York: Modern Library, 2001.

Augustine. *The Confessions*. Translated by Henry Chadwick. New York: Oxford University Press, 2009.

Descartes, René. *Discourse on Method; and, Meditations on First Philosophy*. Miami, FL: BN Publishing, 2007.

Hegel, Georg Wilhelm Friedrich. *Phenomenology of Spirit*. Translated by A. V. Miller. New York: Oxford University Press, 1979.

Kant, Immanuel. *Critique of Pure Reason*. Edited by Marcus Weigelt. New York: Penguin, 2008.

Kierkegaard, Søren. *The Essential Kierkegaard*. Edited by Howard V. Hong and Edna H. Hong. Princeton, NJ: Princeton University Press, 2000.

Locke, John. *Two Treatises of Government*. New York: Everyman, 1993.

Maguire, Jack. *Essential Buddhism: A Complete Guide to Beliefs and Practices*. New York: Atria, 2001.

Marx, Karl. *Selected Writings*. Edited by Lawrence H. Simon. Indianapolis, IN: Hackett, 1994.

Mill, John Stuart, and Jeremy Bentham. *Utilitarianism and Other Essays*. Edited by Alan Ryan. New York: Penguin, 1987.

Nietzsche, Friedrich. *Basic Writings of Nietzsche*. Translated by Walter Kaufmann. New York: Modern Library, 2000.

Plato. *The Republic*. Translated by Desmond Lee. London; New York: Penguin, 2003.

Rand, Ayn. *Atlas Shrugged*. New York: Plume, 1999.

Sartre, Jean-Paul. *Basic Writings*. London; New York: Routledge, 2001.

Smith, Adam. *The Wealth of Nations*. Hollywood, FL: Simon & Brown, 2010.

William of Ockham. *Philosophical Writings*. Indianapolis, IN: Hackett Publishing, 1990.

Index

ꓴAILY BENDEꓤ

Want Some More?

Hit up our humor blog, The Daily Bender, to get your fill of all things funny—be it subversive, odd, offbeat, or just plain mean. The Bender editors are there to get you through the day and on your way to happy hour. Whether we're linking to the latest video that made us laugh or calling out (or bullshit on) whatever's happening, we've got what you need for a good laugh.

If you like our book, you'll love our blog. (And if you hated it, "man up" and tell us why.) Visit The Daily Bender for a shot of humor that'll serve you until the bartender can.

Sign up for our newsletter at

www.adamsmedia.com/blog/humor

and download our Top Ten Maxims No Man Should Live Without.